DISCIPLESHIP

by

ALLEN HADIDIAN

MOODY PRESS
CHICAGO

© 1979, 1987 by
Allen Hadidian

All Scripture quotations, except those noted otherwise, are from the *New American Standard Bible,* © 1960, 1962, 1963, 1968, 1971, 1972, 1973, and 1975 by the Lockman Foundation, and are used by permission.

Library of Congress Cataloging in Publication Data

Hadidian, Allen, 1950-
  Discipleship.

  1. Christian life—1960-   I. Title.
BV4501.2.H24   1987   253   87-1672
ISBN 0-8024-3362-6

1 2 3 4 5 6 7 Printing/BC/Year 92 91 90 89 88 87

Printed in the United States of America

Jerry Myatt and Lynn Cory, this book is dedicated to you, because you two men have been the greatest visible examples to me of the Lord's love for people and of commitment to discipling.

CONTENTS

ACKNOWLEDGMENTS

I am deeply grateful for the contributions that many have made so that this book might become a reality. Larry Paine gave me invaluable help by providing organizational structure for the concepts I had developed. Sandy Scheffler spent many long hours willingly and joyously typing and retyping the manuscript. Calvin and Faith Myatt and Bonnie Van Voorhis helped greatly in the editing of the manuscript. And although her artwork does not appear in this book, I want to thank Carol Smith for developing many special illustrations depicting the discipling concepts, illustrations that I have used when teaching this material in seminars. I am grateful to John MacArthur for his encouragement, support, and faith in me during the writing of the book.

FOREWORD

The apostle John summed up the whole issue of the Christian life and ministry when he said, "The one who says he abides in Him ought himself to walk in the same manner as He walked" (1 John 2:6).

Such an exhortation covers the broadest range of virtues. But for the moment, we can focus on one salient aspect of the walk of the Lord Jesus. He was a "discipler." We know the high priority that He gave to building up disciples. According to the inspired John, we are to be what He was—and that means we are to be disciplers.

Our Lord's commitment to this ministry of discipling can be illustrated from one of the most haunting and insightful truths in the record of our Lord's life, tucked away in semiobscurity in Matthew 27:57. In reference to Joseph of Arimathea, Matthew records: "Who also himself was Jesus' disciple" (KJV). The verb form used indicates the process engaged in by our Lord with Joseph. Jesus discipled Joseph. What a beautiful thought!

The same verb appears once again in Acts 14:21, describing the apostles' ministry in this note: "They had made many disciples." Obviously, they followed Jesus' pattern.

The point is clear. Jesus set a ministry of discipling in motion by the commitment of His own life and the example of the apostolic agents. And He went even further in establishing the importance of discipling. He commanded that we be disciplers when He spoke these final words before His ascension: "Go therefore and make disciples of all the nations" (Matt. 28:19a).

Discipling is the divine strategy for the continuation of the work of Christ. It guarantees the passing on of the patterns and principles of His life. Luke 6:40 sums up the impact of this ministry. There our Lord says, "A pupil is not above his teacher; but ... after he has been fully trained, [he] will be like his teacher." Our Lord wanted to produce a generation like Himself, and discipling others is one means by which we can "walk as He walked."

The book of Acts, which chronicles the continuing work of Christ in His church by the Holy Spirit, begins with the recognition that we must do Jesus' work. "The first account I [Luke] composed, Theophilus, about all that Jesus began to do and teach" (Acts 1:1).

At Grace Community Church, we have been engaged in developing the principles and patterns to make this high calling a reality. The fruit of our discipling ministry has been "exceeding abundantly above all that we ask or think," "thirty, sixty, and a hundredfold." And now the Christian fellowship worldwide can be grateful to the Lord for using the talent and availability of Allen Hadidian to set forth those principles and patterns in a practical, proved way to aid in making the fulfillment of our Lord's mandate a reality. Prior to his becoming pastor/teacher of another congregation in Southern California, I have worked with Allen as a fellow servant at Grace and have seen firsthand the results of the application of those principles. Now I am thrilled that the opportunity for extending them has been made possible.

My prayer is that you will make a commitment to be a discipler, obedient to our Lord's command, eager to follow in His steps to finish what He began.

JOHN MACARTHUR, JR.

1

THE VALUE OF DISCIPLING

One cannot examine the ministry of the Lord Jesus Christ without seeing the emphasis He placed on discipling. It is clear that Jesus' mission was to make provision for the sins of a dying, lost world. He came to seek and save the lost (Luke 19:10). He came that men might believe in Him (John 3:16). How did He reach a lost world? What was His method? Did He start a newspaper service, printing the gospel message so that everyone could read it? Did He write a book explaining why He came? Obviously, neither of these was His approach. Examining the way He spent His time, we see one common thread in the process of His calling and building disciples. Men were His method.

From the very beginning, Christ's strategy of ministry centered on His men. He was always with them—teaching them, training them, encouraging them, rebuking them, and working His ministry in front of them. He was investing in a few men, calling them to be with Him, grounding them in His truths. He invested in those few men so that when He left they could continue the work that He had begun (see Acts 1:1). Men were His method. They became the main focus of His ministry.

After pouring His life into a few men during His ministry on earth, what did Jesus tell His disciples when He was ready to leave? His departing words should have been consistent with His emphasis: training disciples. Listen to what He said to His disciples prior to His ascension:

And Jesus came up and spoke to them, saying, "All authority has been given to Me in heaven and on earth. Go therefore and make

disciples of all the nations, baptizing them in the name of the
Father and the Son and the Holy Spirit, teaching them to observe
all that I commanded you; and lo, I am with you always, even to
the end of the age." (Matthew 28:18-20)

Make disciples. Teach them. He tells us today to continue
the work He began by following the same strategy—that is,
pouring our lives into a few men who can continue His work (2
Timothy 2:2). It is significant that in one of the earliest statements that Jesus made to His men, He did not say, "Follow me
and I will be your friend" (Matthew 4:19). Nor did He say,
"Follow me and I will solve your problems." He did say, "Follow
Me, and I will make you fishers of men." He had a task for them
to accomplish. He called men to Himself so that they could be
equipped to reach a lost world.

Does the value that Christ places on the discipling ministry
affect you? Are you following His example? Are His interests
your interests?

I remember reading the story of a police officer who had a
great desire to see his backyard completely landscaped. He was
shot and killed, however, before he could complete the task.
Some of his fellow officers who had learned to love him donated
their time and money to finish the work their friend had begun.
Because it was the policeman's desire to have it completed, it
became his friends' desire.

What an application that story has for us who love the Lord
Jesus Christ. The discipling ministry was supreme in Christ's life.
He reached the lost with the gospel and reproduced Himself in
men. But the work remains unfinished. Every believer from
Pentecost to "the new heavens and new earth" is engaged in a
monumental task, that of finishing the unfinished work of Christ.
Does your love for Jesus Christ cause you to make His interests
your interests? How much more motivated and compelled to
action we believers should be in working to see the lost saved
and other Christians growing to maturity. Can we show any less
loyalty than the policemen who finished that backyard?

THE VALUE OF DISCIPLING TO THE DISCIPLE

A discipling ministry is of great importance because of its

exceptional value to the disciple.* Unfortunately, most Christians stay in a stage of spiritual immaturity for many years because there is no one to take an interest in their growth in Christ. Because of the many needs and problems new, immature Christians have, it is essential that more mature believers attend personally to them. Every young Christian should be able to say, "Thank You, God, that there is one person who is concerned with my growth in Christ." Every young Christian needs a spiritual guardian. If parents are provided in the physical realm to instruct, train, protect, and provide for the child's growth, it is natural to assume that, in the spiritual realm, those who are more mature are to care for those who are less mature.

The tragedy is that the need is great, but the available disciplers, or spiritual guardians, are few. One fellow told me that if only he had had someone to care personally for him when he first became a Christian, that could have helped him gain victory over a drug involvement. He realizes that he was responsible for his own actions, but I could not help but think of the number of Christians who are struggling with sin because there is no one who is willing to show personal concern. Another man said that he became a Christian at age thirteen and no one took responsibility to give him guidance until thirteen years later!

How is a discipling ministry valuable in the life of the disciple?

DISCIPLING INCREASES THE RATE OF THE DISCIPLE'S GROWTH

When a person becomes a Christian, he enters a new life in which growth is essential and should be constant. The consistent, personal attention given him by a discipler can only increase the rate of this process of spiritual growth.[1]

Imagine the benefit of knowing a mature Christian who desired to spend time with you, guiding and directing your life. That person would be able to encourage you when you were depressed and teach you biblical principles that would help you develop spiritual habits. If I were a new or young Christian, I would want to meet with someone who was more mature than I

---

*Throughout this book, the term *disciple* refers to a disciple of the Lord rather than to the discipler's "disciple."

1. Gary W. Kuhne, *The Dynamics of Personal Follow-Up* (Grand Rapids, Zondervan, 1976), pp. 20-21.

so that I could reach the goal of maturity faster. It seems only logical. If a person wants to be an effective artist, he should spend time with someone who is a competent artist. His mastery of the skill would increase much faster that way than if he learned by trial and error. There are many Christians in the Body of Christ whose rate of spiritual growth would increase if they entered into a discipling relationship. Is there one person you know who is less mature than you are who could benefit from your love and concern?

DISCIPLING STOPS WRONG BEHAVIORAL PATTERNS IN THE DISCIPLE

We are creatures of habit, and it is unfortunate but true that we can continue living in habit patterns that are displeasing to God after we have become Christians. A Christian may be unaware that such behavior can eventually bring serious chastening if not corrected. The Christian just coming out of the old life needs to understand that because he is now a new man in Christ, certain patterns of living need to be changed. The loving and gentle correction of a mature believer can give him the guidance he needs.[2]

This same kind of correction is seen in athletics. A good coach will observe his players and point out problems and bad habits in their form and execution. A tennis coach will notice that a player's toss of the ball during the serve needs correcting. I know of a high school track runner who lacked knowledge on how to prepare adequately for a race, and consequently she could not run her best. Someone coached her privately and put a stop to the wrong preparation patterns. In her next race, she finished higher than she ever had before.

Perhaps when you were a new Christian, no one took time to lovingly correct some of your wrong patterns of living. Think how much sooner victory would have taken place in your life if someone had cared. Then think of those Christians around you who need your help and who would love to overcome wrong behavioral patterns.

2. Ibid., p. 20.

DISCIPLING PROTECTS THE DISCIPLE

A third way in which a discipler's ministry is valuable in the life of the disciple is that it gives the disciple protection from the attacks of the enemy.[3] An immature Christian is more likely to be defeated by Satan than a more mature Christian who is similarly attacked. It is easy for the immature Christian to believe Satan's lies, doubting his salvation or questioning God's love and forgiveness. He can become easily discouraged when he fails to gain mastery over recurring sin. Many times I have talked to new Christians who think that God has stopped loving them because they commit the same sins over and over again.

The problem is that immature Christians have not built up any resistance to Satan's attacks. Satan's attacks can be compared to a disease. Until the body has built up resistance to a disease, it is very susceptible to that disease. The new Christian is likewise susceptible to Satan's attacks.

How does a new Christian build up spiritual resistance? He develops it in the Word of God. Unfortunately, the immature Christian has very little knowledge of the Word of God, which makes him defenseless. Thus the immature Christian can be compared to a quarterback with no blockers. Ephesians 6:13 says, "Take up the full armor of God, that you may be able to resist," but the new Christian has very little armor. In a sense, he is practically naked. He has the helmet of salvation and a very tiny shield of faith, but that is about it. That is why discipling is so important. The discipler is spiritually dressing up the immature Christian.

Somewhere in your sphere of relationships, there is a believer who is weaker and less knowledgeable than you who needs your protective love. The victories that you have won through your insight into the Word of God need to be explained to less mature, struggling Christians. Are you willing to commit yourself to them so that they can learn to walk consistently with God?

DISCIPLING PROVIDES THE DISCIPLE WITH A PERSONAL FRIEND

When a person becomes a believer in Jesus Christ, he can feel somewhat isolated. He realizes that his old manner of life,

3. Ibid., pp. 19-20.

encouraged by association with his friends, is no longer acceptable to God, and thus his tendency is to slowly withdraw from his non-Christian friends. Unless he consistently spends time with a Christian who can meet his spiritual and social needs, however, he may move back to his old friends, compromising his Christian testimony and eventually losing all desire for spiritual matters. A discipling ministry provides the disciple with a close, personal friend.

DISCIPLING PROVIDES THE DISCIPLE WITH COUNSEL

Many immature Christians get involved in questionable activities, or else they make decisions that turn out to be wrong, simply because they do not have that one person to whom they can go to seek counsel. In a discipling relationship, that one person is available. The many questions and problems that arise for the disciple need the wisdom and insight of someone more mature than the disciple himself.

THE VALUE OF DISCIPLING TO THE DISCIPLER

We have discussed briefly the value of discipling to Christ and the disciple. Now we shall consider the value to the one doing the discipling. Whenever a person is obedient to God's commands, he receives personal benefit and blessing in return. This is clearly true in a discipling ministry.

DISCIPLING BRINGS JOY TO THE DISCIPLER

God has used the men I have discipled to bring incredible joy to my life. What a privilege it is to watch those in God's family grow. What a privilege to watch them mature in their prayer life and learn truths from the Bible. What a joy to watch them struggle with sin and then become victorious. The apostles John and Paul expressed this joy clearly:

> I have no greater joy than this, to hear of my children walking in the truth. (3 John 4)

> For who is our hope or joy or crown of exultation? Is it not even you, in the presence of our Lord Jesus at His coming? For you are our glory and joy. (1 Thessalonians 2:19-20)

For what thanks can we render to God for you in return for all the joy with which we rejoice before our God on your account? (1 Thessalonians 3:9)

Several years ago, I met a very special individual who became one of the most faithful men I have had the privilege of discipling. One day I expressed to him the joy he had brought to my life. About a year later he came to me and said, "Allen, I could not understand what you meant when you said I brought you joy. But now I'm discipling Dave, and I can't believe the joy he's brought to my life." Many times after meeting with the men I was discipling, I went to the Lord in thanksgiving for all the joy He brought to my life through them. Do you know the unique joy of discipling others?

DISCIPLING PURIFIES THE LIFE OF THE DISCIPLER

Discipling others has a purifying effect on the discipler. God is in the business of bringing us into conformity with His Son, and He will use many things to accomplish that: trials, the Word, people, ministry, and circumstances. God has caused certain weaknesses in my life to become apparent to me as I have become involved in discipling ministries. I did not know how impatient I was until I started getting involved with people. I did not know how harsh and insensitive I could be until I started getting involved with people. A discipler may be shocked at what he learns about himself when he concentrates on someone else.

One matures as he ministers. Although it is true that one does not assume a discipler's role until certain qualities are present in his life, it is also true that as one begins discipling, God builds into the discipler godly qualities. Thus another value of discipling others is the purification that takes place in the life of the discipler.

DISCIPLING DEVELOPS MINISTERIAL SKILLS IN THE DISCIPLER

A discipler will learn how to teach the disciple. He will learn the mechanics of counseling. He will learn how to guide someone into a ministry. He will learn how to lead a discussion. These and many other skills that expand his capability in ministry are developed in the discipler's life.

DISCIPLING PROVIDES AN OUTLET FOR THE DISCIPLER

It is very easy for Christians to become reservoirs of knowledge with no output. When that occurs, the Christian is like the stagnant Dead Sea—rich, but flowing nowhere. Working with a less mature Christian provides the outlet the discipler needs for teaching the many truths he is learning. By passing on what he knows, the discipler stays fresh.

THE VALUE OF DISCIPLING TO THE CHURCH

Not only is a discipling ministry important because of Christ's example and its value to the disciple and discipler, but it also has great value to the church. The discipling ministry strengthens the church body and perpetuates God's work by developing godly leaders for the church. The church has always desperately needed young, strong leaders. It is usually those who have been discipled and directed into a ministry who rise to some level of leadership. On the other hand, where there is no discipling, there is loss. Chuck Miller, a seminar speaker on Christian discipling, says that discipling involves carrying on the plan of God without a "break in the cadence." The result of discipling is that God's work will continue in future generations. If we do not disciple, there is no guarantee that a ministry will continue. That is what 2 Timothy 2:2 is all about. In essence, Paul was saying, "Timothy, there should not be a break in the cadence of God's work. You find men who are faithful and to whom you can pass the baton."

J. Edwin Orr in his book *Campus Aflame* (Glendale, Calif.: Regal, 1972) discusses the history of the first 113 colleges and universities in America. Do you know *why* institutions such as Dartmouth, Princeton, Harvard, and Yale were founded? They were to be colleges for preachers. What happened to those schools that began with a strong Christian foundation? Somewhere the discipling process stopped, and now we are facing the consequences. Somewhere along the line, the men in the universities failed to pass on the baton. It was just a matter of time before the schools drifted away from their Christian base.

The YMCA was founded as a weeknight Bible study by George Williams in London in the middle of the 1800s. Here, too, a strong, evangelical Christian base existed. But again, as time went by the *C* vanished. Again, someone forgot to disciple. Someone forgot to take what God was doing to him, reproduce it in people of another generation, and enable them to reproduce it in a third generation. The tragedy of not discipling is evident.

If the church is to continue as a strong, dynamic, working fellowship of believers who adhere to and perpetuate the truth, the ministry of discipling others is essential.

THE VALUE OF DISCIPLING TO THE WORLD

My greatest desire is to be used by God to change the world for Jesus Christ. One of the greatest spiritual mysteries is that God uses men like me to accomplish such a goal. And if the world ever needed changing, it needs it now. I want to change this world where I can. I want to have an impact. I do not want written on my tombstone, "He came, he stayed, he left." Therefore, at one point I had to evaluate my life and goals and ask myself the questions, What am I doing that can ultimately have an impact on this world? What am I doing that will have eternal consequences?

But what is eternal? If you were to do a study on this question, you would find that three things are eternal. First, God is eternal. "The eternal God is a dwelling place" (Deuteronomy 33:27). Second, the Word of God is eternal. "The grass withers, the flower fades, but the word of our God stands forever" (Isaiah 40:8). Third, people are eternal. "Do not marvel at this; for an hour is coming, in which all who are in the tombs shall hear His voice, and shall come forth; those who did the good deeds, to a resurrection of life, those who committed the evil deeds, to a resurrection of judgment" (John 5:28-29). These verses state that everyone will come forth. Everyone will live forever. Some will live eternally in God's presence, and some will live and be eternally separate from God.

In light of this study, nothing motivates and challenges me more than to see *people's* eternal lives changed by the eternal *Word of God* so that *God's* eternal life can be made manifest. That is why I agree with Warren Webster, a missionary to Pakistan, who made this statement at an InterVarsity conference: "If I had my life to live over again, I would live it to change the lives of men. Because you haven't changed anything until you've changed the lives of men."

How are you going to use your time, knowledge, and ability? Will you use it on that which is temporal or on that which is eternal? How satisfying it will be when we are close to death to know that we are leaving behind other people who, committed to God, His Word, and His people, are carrying out the work that we have entrusted to them.

2
THE DEFINITION OF DISCIPLING

The problem in defining discipling is that the Bible does not give us a one-statement description. We have taken a biblical term, "disciple," and turned it into a gerund, *discipling*. We have then taken that term and used it to describe many kinds of relationships and activities. But even though we cannot go to just one passage of the Bible to get a complete definition of a discipling ministry, we can gain some insight as we examine the outworking of God's plan for the individual and the identifying marks of a discipling ministry. Once we have done that a complete definition will surface.

We can begin to define discipling by recognizing that the discipling process brings about the fulfillment of three desires that God has for each individual. There is a corresponding operation in a discipling ministry for each of these three desires of God. We shall call these operations "phases."

PHASE 1: EVANGELIZING MEN

God's first desire for men is that they come to a saving knowledge of Jesus Christ. He desires that all men repent and be reconciled to Him (2 Peter 3:9). He sent His Son so that men might believe and receive eternal life (John 3:16). Because His desire is that men be saved, the first phase in a discipling ministry is evangelism or winning people to Christ. We see this in Matthew 28:19, where Jesus tells us to "go therefore and make disciples of all the nations." When Jesus says to make disciples, He is telling us to first go and "make believers"— evangelize.

We see support for this understanding of "make disciples" in Acts 14:21. Paul and Barnabas were in Derbe on their first missionary journey, "and after they had preached the gospel to

that city and had made many disciples, they returned to Lystra
and to Iconium and to Antioch." In other words, Paul preached
the gospel, many believed, and when they received the gospel
message into their lives they became disciples.

So Matthew 28:19 is telling us to go and make believers out
of unbelievers. Go and evangelize. Win people to Christ. We are
also told to go into all the world and preach the gospel (Mark
16:15), proclaiming Christ's name to all the nations (Luke 24:47).

The task of evangelism can also be seen as begetting spiritual children. Just as Paul referred to Onesimus as his "child"
(Philemon 10), so we should be able in the same way to refer to
those whom we have led to Christ and nurtured in faith. Seeing
people come to Christ for salvation is God's desire, Paul's pattern, and the emphasis with which we are to begin a discipling
ministry.

But evangelism is not an end in itself. God's plan for the
individual does not stop with salvation. That is the initial phase,
serving as a means to the next phase.

PHASE 2: EDIFYING MEN

Once a person has become a believer, God desires that he
grow to spiritual maturity. God is not interested in having believers remain spiritual children, but rather He desires that they
grow to be strong, young men (1 John 2:13) and fathers (1 John
2:14). Consequently, the second phase in a discipling ministry is
the edification, or building up, of those who are saved. This
phase emphasizes the nurturing of the person's growth in Christ—
teaching him, strengthening him, encouraging him, admonishing him, and exhorting him. To edify is to build up a person in
his walk with Christ until Christ is formed in him (Galatians
4:19). Because He knows the importance of edification, Christ
tells us that after we have made many disciples—that is, believers—
we are to be "teaching them to observe all that I commanded
you" (Matthew 28:20).

John MacArthur points out the importance of the second
phase of discipling in the following statements:

> What is a discipler? Somebody who goes, baptizes—that means wins
> somebody to Christ—teaches—that means builds them up.

How do you make a disciple? You go to somebody who isn't one. You win them to Jesus Christ and you teach them all things "whatsoever I have commanded." You build them in the Word. That's the job that all of us have.[1]

Also aware of the importance of edification, Paul and Barnabas, after they had "made disciples" in Lystra, Iconium, and Antioch, did not stop with phase 1. They became involved in phase 2. We notice in Acts 14:21-22 that they returned to those cities, strengthening the souls of the disciples, encouraging them to continue in the faith. That is what phase 2 is all about—building someone to maturity.

Still God's desire for the individual does not stop with maturity. Maturity becomes an intermediate step to another desire of God, which is seen in the last phase.

PHASE 3: EQUIPPING MEN

To God, salvation and maturity are not enough. He desires that men become spiritual reproducers. If our job in phase 1 is to evangelize men and our job in phase 2 is to edify men, then our job in phase 3 is to equip men so that they can be sent out to reproduce themselves in others.

We saw in chapter 1 that that was Christ's strategy—reproducing His life in His men and equipping them so that they could continue His work by reproducing their lives in others. Because that was His strategy, Jesus told the Father that having taught the disciples, He was then going to send them into the world (John 17:18), as the Father had sent Him (John 20:21).

As we see in Christ's example, the concept of discipling others involved in phase 3 points to the sending out of mature individuals who are equipped to reproduce their lives in others. As you can see, discipling involves building into the lives of not only the present spiritual generations, but also into the lives of future spiritual generations.

The entire discipling process is very much analogous to physical life. Phase 1 (evangelizing) is the birth of the child. Phase 2 (edifying) is the rearing of the child. Phase 3 (equipping)

1. John MacArthur, "The Call and Qualities of a Discipler," Acts 14:1-28, tape 1243, Grace Community Church, 13248 Roscoe Blvd., Sun Valley, CA 91352.

is the sending out of the person who is now old enough and able to bear and rear others. Each of these three phases is important. They must all work together for the biblical concept of discipling others to be realized.

Having seen the three phases, we still are not ready to present a complete definition of a discipling ministry. We need to get more specific by examining the identifying marks of a discipling relationship. How can a discipling ministry be distinguished from other ministries? What are the ingredients of a discipling ministry that set it apart from other kinds of ministries? Let's look at seven identifying marks of such a ministry and then state the complete definition of discipling others.

MARK 1: GUARDIANSHIP

In a discipling relationship, the discipler is the spiritual guardian of the disciple. The discipler is overseeing the spiritual walk of the person. *Overseer* literally means "one who watches over," which best explains guardianship. Thus the discipler is watching over the disciple and his growth. Hebrews 13:17, speaking of leaders, expresses this idea:"Obey your leaders, and submit to them; for they *keep watch over your souls,* as those who will give an account" (emphasis added).

One of the men I discipled said during a prayer, "Thank You, God, for sending Allen to me to watch over me." That's the idea!

Being a guardian means giving direction and guidance to the disciple's life. It means counseling him, praying for him, training him, and teaching him. It means watching out for things in his life that can harm him. It means warning him. All of these are essential elements in the role of a guardian.

Being a guardian is having the attitude that God has entrusted to your care a person, and for that reason you are that person's spiritual guardian. In a sense, it is the assuming of a parent-child relationship with a new believer. Paul said in 1 Thessalonians 2 that the things he did to the Thessalonians were the things that a father would do to his own children. Guardianship means giving parental care to your "child" until he is able to stand on his own. How desperately a young Christian needs a spiritual guardian who will watch over him and help him during those early stages of his spiritual development.

How evident this identifying mark was in Christ's life. He was the Master Guardian. He was always looking after the disciples, like a shepherd watching over the sheep in his flock. He was guiding them, protecting them from harm, and counseling them. He never allowed them to stray too far without words of warning. When they became discouraged, He always brought them encouraging words. His life was the perfect example of what a guardian ought to do.

MARK 2: EXAMPLE

The discipler as a godly example is another identifying mark of a discipling relationship. In a discipling ministry, there are the roles of the leader and the follower, the guide and the guided. The discipler is being watched and listened to by the disciple. This means, of course, that the discipler must have a life worth reproducing, a life that is worthy of being watched. This does not mean that he must live a perfect life. No one but the Lord Jesus did that. Rather, he must reach a point in his walk with Christ at which he has something to impart to younger believers.

Have you reached the point of having something to pass on to a new Christian? If you have, look around you. There is probably someone who needs you and desperately needs to learn the things you have learned. There is someone who needs to be loved and cared for by you. There is someone who wants to watch your life and follow your example. Pray that God would point out that person to you.

MARK 3: DIRECTION

In a discipling ministry, there are clearly defined goals and a plan to achieve those goals. There are specific objectives. We see this in Christ's ministry. As mentioned earlier, Jesus' calling of His men to a relationship with Him was a calling to a goal and a task. He said, "Follow me, and I will make you fishers of men" (Matthew 4:19).

When the discipler meets with the disciples, he needs to have his goals in mind. There needs to be that sense of direction. He does not want to be just getting together with the disciple and "seeing what happens."

Many years ago, when I was on staff with a Christian organization I was discipling some young men. The person who was training me said, "Allen, what are you doing with these men? Where are you taking them? What are your goals for them?"

"I don't know," I said. "I'm just meeting with them and sharing a few truths with them."

"Allen," he said, "you need to think through how to bring them to a level of maturity."

After that conversation, I knew I had some serious thinking to do. *How do I bring a young Christian to the point of maturity? What are the goals I should have for his life, and how do I get him there?* Those are the kinds of questions one asks when thinking through the principle of direction.

Because the discipler has goals that need to be reached in the disciple's life, a discipling relationship is characterized by a consistent, personal, organized time with the disciple. This is certainly not to say that there will not be times that are informal. Those times are extremely valuable. However, because he has goals in mind, the discipler will want to impart content, knowledge, and skills to the young Christian. That impartation requires planned, personal, and consistently held meetings.

MARK 4: TIME

We have seen that guardianship, example, and direction are identifying marks in a discipling relationship. A fourth mark is the commitment of time. A discipling ministry requires a long-term commitment, not just a short-term commitment. Look at the life of Christ. He spent several years with the same men. I am not implying that a disciple needs to spend two or three years with those whom he disciples, although he might. But the commitment is certainly not short term.

We must get away from the idea that discipling someone is something you do for eight or ten weeks. Many people confuse a discipling ministry with a ten-week basic Bible doctrine course. They think that after the ten weeks are over, they have sufficiently discipled a person. Teaching a ten-week course is not discipling someone. Such a course will probably be a part of discipling an individual, but there is more to discipling than that. Discipling is a long-term commitment to a person. It is spending time with him until he is able to stand on his own and begin a ministry in the life of someone else. So, the fourth identifying mark is the commitment of time.

MARK 5: COMMITMENT OF ONE'S LIFE

In Christ's relationship with His disciples, we do not see Him *just* relating spiritual truths to them. We see Him investing His life in them. He was committed to them. When He told them to follow Him, He was implying that He would stay close to them and be committed to them. Thus another identifying mark of a discipling relationship is the commitment of one's life to another. This commitment is not simply the transferring of facts but rather the transferring of one's life to another. It involves a person-to-person, face-to-face encounter. It is an act of the will, a giving of oneself sacrificially to the young Christian. Are you willing to give of yourself in that way?

MARK 6: NUMERICAL LIMITATION

Observing Christ's ministry, we note that He had a multitude of people following Him, and from that multitude seventy men were chosen. From the seventy, twelve were appointed; and out of the twelve, He had an inner circle of three with whom He became deeply involved. His most intense involvement was with a few people. From this we learn that a discipling ministry has numerical limits. Because time and the commitment of one's life to the disciple are essential elements in discipling someone, the discipler must set his own limits on the number of individuals he will disciple. He might be able to be committed to one or two people, or possibly four or five. Available time, his own maturity in the Lord, and his experience in discipling will probably determine the number of young Christians he will disciple.

MARK 7: FRIENDSHIP

One of the beautiful qualities about Christ's relationship with His disciples was that even though He was their leader, guardian, and adviser, He was also their friend. In John 15:14 He says, "You are My friends." In Luke 12:4 He says, "And I say to you, My friends." One of the joyous ingredients in a discipling relationship is the building of a friendship with the brother or sister you are discipling. I cannot emphasize this enough. Thomas Kehn, in his excellent unpublished seminary thesis, stated it very well:

> The discipler is not a part-time tutor; he is a full-time friend.
>
> The discipler is not someone who walks into a person's life for a few hours a week of instruction and then disappears until class adjoins again. No, the discipler is to be one who takes a genuine interest in the one he is personally leading. He spends time with him doing a myriad of things—some serious, others fun and light-hearted, some formal, others casual. The discipler becomes a true friend to his young convert.[2]

The men I have discipled looked to me as the guardian of their lives, as someone from whom to seek counsel. I looked at them as men to be nurtured in Christ. But our relationship went much deeper than that. Those brothers became my friends. I enjoyed being with them and doing things with them. We supported one another and were loyal to each other. We cared for each other, and our friendship grew. One of the men I discipled repaired my car engine. He not only spent much time on it, but he paid for all the parts! I thanked him repeatedly for it, and his reply was, "Allen, that is what friendship is all about!"

Someone once asked me, "How much time do you spend with the men you are discipling?"

I responded, "At least one hour a week."

But I thought more about the question later and realized that I did not think about it in those terms, as if I had a set amount of time. It was just natural for me to spend time with them because they were my friends.

I emphasize friendship with the disciple lest you think that a discipling relationship is a cold, mechanical, and structured ministry. Please do not misunderstand. As you read through the remaining chapters, it could appear that discipling is nothing more than putting a person through a formal program, like a car through an assembly line. That is the farthest thing from my

2. Thomas Kehn, "The Ministry of Youth Discipleship: Its Questions and Answers," Master's thesis, Talbot Theological Seminary, 1975, p. 63.

mind. Discipling involves building a relationship with someone, a friendship. Friendship, then, is the last identifying mark of a discipling relationship.

COMPLETE DEFINITION

Having looked at the three phases of a discipling ministry and the identifying marks, let's put together a complete definition of discipling others. We will incorporate in the definition the three phases and six of the seven marks (friendship being excluded). The following definition will be used throughout the remaining chapters:

	Discipling others is the process
	by which a Christian with a
Example	life worth emulating
Commitment	commits himself
Time	for an extended period of time
Numerical	to a few individuals
Limitation	who have been
Phase 1	*won to Christ,* the
Direction	purpose being to
Guardianship	aid and guide their
Phase 2	*growth to maturity* and equip them to
Phase 3	*reproduce themselves* in a third spiritual
	generation.

Notice that discipling begins with a life worth emulating and that it is aimed at a third spiritual generation.

Before continuing in the book, one thought needs to be expressed. As we just discussed, the term *discipling others* involves the work of evangelism. But because the content of this material is geared toward working with Christians, when I use the term *discipling* in the remaining chapters, my emphasis will be on phases 2 and 3, that is, on maturity and reproduction. This material is not intended to be a course of evangelism, but rather a discussion on how to nurture immature Christians to a point of maturity at which they can multiply their lives into others.

3
GOALS IN DISCIPLING

In a discipling ministry, it is essential that you know your goal. Someone has said, "If you aim at nothing, you're sure to hit it." A discipler cannot afford to aim at nothing.

As a discipler, you need to ask yourself the question, Why am I discipling? What am I doing with the disciples? Let's look at the goals of a discipling ministry as they are stated in the definition of discipling others:

> Discipling others is the process
> by which a Christian with a life worth emulating
> commits himself for an extended period of time
> to a few individuals who have been
> won to Christ, the
> purpose being to
> aid and guide their
> *growth to maturity and equip them to*
> *reproduce themselves in a third spiritual generation.*

The last two lines direct us to the goals in discipling others—maturity and multiplication. Let's examine those two goals.

GOAL 1: PEOPLE WHO ARE MATURE

The first goal in a discipling ministry is to develop people who are mature. In Colossians 1:28 Paul says, "And we proclaim Him, admonishing every man and teaching every man with all wisdom, that we may present every man complete in Christ." The word translated "complete" is *teleios* in the Greek, and it refers to that which is perfect, or mature.

The Greek word translated "present" is from the same Greek root word as the word translated "present" in Romans 12:1,

"Present your bodies a living and holy sacrifice," and Romans 6:13, "Present . . . your members as instruments of righteousness to God." The word means "to offer, or put at one's disposal," and it is the same word that was used in the Septuagint* to signify the presenting of Levitical victims and offerings before the Lord so that He could show His approval. So Paul's goal, which should be the goal of every discipler, was to be able to place before the Lord people of whom He could approve, that is, mature people.

The word *teleios* is also used in Ephesians 4:13, speaking of the maturing of the Body of Christ: "Until we all attain to the unity of the faith, and of the knowledge of the Son of God, to a mature man, to the measure of the stature which belongs to the fulness of Christ."

Examining this Greek term even more closely, we find that in secular writing it was used to refer to heirs being *of age*, to four *full-grown* cocks, to acacia trees being in *good condition*, and to a mill that was *in good working condition*. In the Septuagint, *teleios* is translated "unblemished, undivided, complete, whole, and blameless."[1] Abbott-Smith points out that its meaning in the New Testament is "having reached its end, finished, mature, complete, perfect."[2] Thus the basic thoughts behind the New Testament idea of maturity are those of completeness, wholeness, being full-grown, lacking nothing, and being fully developed.

How does maturity relate to the Christian life? As Christians, we are striving for wholeness, full development, completeness. The apostle Paul was certainly progressing toward maturity (Philippians 3:12), and he desired that others progress with him. But what exactly is a mature person? Let's look at five marks of a mature person. Gary W. Kuhne has been helpful to me in this area.[3]

---

*The Septuagint is the Greek translation of the Old Testament.
1. James Hope Moulton and George Milligan, *The Vocabulary of the Greek Testament* (Grand Rapids, Mich.: Eerdmans, 1949), p. 629.
2. G. Abbott-Smith, *A Manual Greek Lexicon of the New Testament*, 3d ed. (New York: Scribner's, n.d.), p. 442.
3. Gary W. Kuhne, *The Dynamics of Personal Follow-up* (Grand Rapids, Mich.: Zondervan, 1976), pp. 73-74.

MARK 1: CHRISTLIKE IN CHARACTER

Ephesians 4:13 says that we are to grow "to a mature man, to the measure of the stature which belongs to the fulness of Christ." "Stature" refers to the growth of a man, and the man we Christians are to grow to be like is the Lord Jesus Christ. He is our standard and model. A mature man is one who manifests Christlike qualities in his life.

What more perfectly explains Christlikeness in character than Galatians 5:22–23: "But the fruit of the Spirit is love, joy, peace, patience, kindness, goodness, faithfulness, gentleness, self-control; against such things there is no law." Those nine qualities were perfectly displayed in Christ. If those whom you disciple are to be conformed to His image, it should be your goal to see those qualities manifested in their lives.

MARK 2: DEPENDENCE ON CHRIST

On a human level, how do we recognize maturity? Maturity is seen as an individual goes from a state of complete dependence on parents to a state of independence from parents—he becomes able to take care of himself and make his own decisions. In the spiritual realm, maturity is seen in the progression from independence from God to dependence on God. Before we knew God, we were independent of Him, rebellious, and trusting in ourselves. But when we received Christ we became dependent on Him, and that dependence should be continually increasing. That is the process that is seen in any person who is growing in his relationship with God.

Abraham certainly learned to trust God. "With respect to the promise of God, he did not waver in unbelief, but grew strong in faith" (Romans 4:20). Paul also knew the reality of Christ being his life. In Galatians 2:20 he says that Christ lived in him and that his life was lived by faith in Christ. To Paul, Christ was the source of every activity, his very life. Paul's desire is most evident in Philippians 3:10. Paul wanted to "know Him, and the power of His resurrection and the fellowship of His sufferings." It was an intimate acquaintance with Christ's person, power, and pain that was foremost in Paul's desires. A mark of maturity, therefore, is an ever increasing dependence on Jesus Christ.

MARK 3: INDEPENDENT OF OTHERS

Whereas dependence is necessary when Christ is the object, independence is essential when thinking in terms of one's need for close spiritual supervision by others. A person is spiritually mature when he is at the point in his life at which he no longer is completely dependent on other Christians for his spiritual growth. Some time ago, I was meeting with an individual who said to me, "Allen, I need you to challenge me and watch over me." We met regularly, but after a while we stopped getting together. Why? He came to a point beyond which he did not need that constant challenge and motivation from me. He became independent of me. I know that this has been true in my own life. As I grow in my dependency on Christ, I do not have to depend on people as much as I used to. That certainly is not saying that people are unimportant. They are, but I do not have to depend constantly on them. John MacArthur summarized this aspect of spiritual maturity very clearly:

> I'd say a mature Christian is a Christian who is self-motivated. In other words, he is outside the necessity of being cranked up by somebody else. . . . He is enough plugged into the power of the Lord and sensitive to the Lord that he is motivated by his relationship to Christ apart from anybody else having to be superficially motivating him.[4]

Think of Christ's life. Were other people *essential* to His walk with God? They definitely were not! He was independently dependent on the Father. Again, that is not saying that He did not like people, see value in them, or benefit from their unique giftedness. But as far as His walk with the Father was concerned, people were not essential. When people were available, He wanted their help. He asked some of His disciples to pray as He was in the Garden of Gethsemane, but they failed. Christ was dependent on the Father and independent of others.

The same must be true in the disciple's life. Quoting again from Thomas Kehn's thesis:

4. Jerry Romano, "Church Growth Report—Grace Community Church of the Valley," paper for course titled "Social Structure and Church Growth II," Jan. 14, 1975, Biola College.

The purpose behind discipling others is not to pacify and to accommodate the spiritual baby until his Heavenly Father returns for him. The discipler should be assisting the person to become basically free and independent of him as a continual overseer. This does not mean that all ties are severed, not at all. But he should lead the person to become independently-dependent upon Christ.[5]

In Acts 20:32, Paul is giving his last words to the elders from Ephesus. He says, "And now I commend you to God and to the word of His grace." Paul had taught those men for several years, and he knew they had reached the point beyond which they could be independent from him. All they needed were two things: the Lord of the Word and the Word of the Lord. Paul said, in essence, "You don't need me. I have taught you the whole counsel of God, and now you are able to take the baton and run with it." That is what maturity is.

MARK 4: CONSISTENCY OF WALK

Was Christ's life consistent? Absolutely! Jesus said, "I always do the things that are pleasing to Him" (John 8:29). Consistent perfection characterized His life. How does consistency of walk relate to us? Kuhne defines consistency as an "overall direction of visible growth in a Christian's life in spite of periodic stumbling."[6] In other words, even though a Christian will fall at times, the pattern of his life is one of positive growth. His life is characterized by a commitment to the basics of Christian growth. For example, he deals continually with sin in his life and with living the Spirit-filled life. He has a continual intake of the Word, and he knows how to apply the Word to problems in his life. The apostle Paul realized the importance of a consistent life. In Philippians 3:16 he says, "However, let us keep living by that same standard to which we have attained." In other words, walk consistently with what you have learned.

MARK 5: STABILITY DUE TO A CLEAR UNDERSTANDING
OF BIBLICAL TRUTH

"As a result, we are no longer to be children, tossed here and there by waves, and carried about by every wind of doctrine,

5. Thomas Kehn, "The Ministry of Youth Discipleship: Its Questions and Answers," Master's thesis, Talbot Theological Seminary, 1975, pp. 55-56.
6. Kuhne, p. 135.

by the trickery of men, by craftiness in deceitful scheming" (Ephesians 4:14). Paul said that we are not to be like children, who are easily influenced by others and thus very unstable ("tossed here and there by waves"). He also said we are not to be "carried about by every wind of doctrine." The picture is of a vessel that is being tossed around with every wind and thus has no settled line of sailing. An immature person, a child, has no fixed views of doctrines that are settled in his mind, and thus he is vulnerable to every new opinion. A mature person is one who has acquired settled views of the truth and is able to discern false teaching (Acts 20:29-31; 2 Corinthians 11:13-15; Colossians 2:8).

Many people involved in a discipling ministry, however, see maturity as the *only* goal and fail to recognize the importance of the second goal.

GOAL 2: PEOPLE WHO ARE MULTIPLIERS

What is a multiplier? A multiplier is a person who is committed to the task of reproducing his life in someone else, who in turn will reproduce himself in a third spiritual generation.

A multiplicative ministry can best be described as a chain effect. The following diagram pictures it:

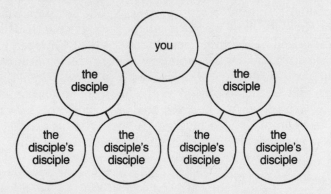

"You" are the first generation, "the disciple" is the second generation, and "the disciple's disciple" is the third generation.

EXAMPLES OF MULTIPLICATION

Several Scripture passages clearly show the multiplication process. Second Timothy 2:2 says, "And the things which you have heard from me in the presence of many witnesses, these entrust to faithful men, who will be able to teach others also." How many generations are represented in this verse? Four! Second Timothy 2:2 could be charted like this:

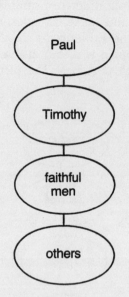

First Thessalonians 1:6-8 shows this picture:

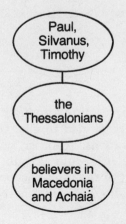

Paul, Silvanus, and Timothy became examples to the Thessalonians who followed them, and the Thessalonians sounded forth the

Word of God to the people in Macedonia and Achaia. The result was that many believed. What a dramatic impact the Thessalonians had!

Combined, Matthew 28:18-20 and Acts 8:26-39 reveal another picture of multiplication. Jesus ministered to the disciples, who were told to go and make disciples. One of their converts was Philip, who led the Ethiopian eunuch to Christ. Tradition tells us that this Ethiopian was responsible for the establishment of the Christian church in Africa. The picture would look something like this:

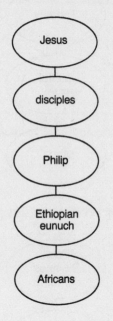

Many other examples of the multiplication process could be given. One person I know said that he could trace his spiritual roots back ten generations. Another person said that at one point in his ministry, he could account for more than forty people who were part of the multiplication chain of his life. He had discipled a few, who discipled others, who in turn discipled still others.

One remarkable example of multiplication in action is the story of Dawson Trotman, founder of the Navigators, and Les

Spencer, a navy man.[7] After Trotman had been teaching Spencer truths from God's Word for some time, Spencer brought a friend from his ship to Trotman and said, "Dawson, I want you to teach him all you have taught me."

But Dawson said, "I am not going to teach him; you are going to teach him. If you cannot teach him what I have taught you, then I have failed."

Les Spencer began to teach his friend, and the multiplication process began. Spencer's friend eventually found someone else who needed to be taught, and the process continued until on that one ship there were one hundred twenty-five men meeting every week for prayer and Bible study. Those men then went to other ships and bases until, at the height of World War II, there were groups of believers started by these men on more than one thousand ships and naval bases all over the world.

Eventually the FBI heard about those groups with no name or charter, and it began to investigate. When agents went to one person and asked how the group got started, the reply would be, "I don't know. I met someone on another ship who started a group." So, the FBI agents went to that person with their questions, only to be referred to another person on another ship. The investigation continued for three months until they were finally able to trace the whole ministry back to Dawson Trotman. That is how the Navigators got started. That is multiplication!

My purpose in relating these examples is not to cater to your pride but rather to your imagination. The impact the multiplication principle can have is exciting. Look at all the people whose lives have been touched. I hope that now you can see why a discipling ministry is so essential (chap. 1) and so personally satisfying. Every person a disciple spends time with is an extension of the discipler's ministry.

EXPLOSIVENESS OF MULTIPLICATION

Walter Henrichsen, personnel director for the Navigators, suggests a hypothetical situation in his book *Disciples Are Made— Not Born*, that clearly illustrates the process of multiplication.[8]

7. Jim White, "Endurance in the Great Commission," cassette. The Navigators, P.O. Box 20, Colorado Springs, CO 80901.
8. Walter A. Henrichsen, *Disciples Are Made—Not Born* (Wheaton, Ill.: Victor, 1974), p. 142.

Suppose a father offers his two sons the choice of taking either one dollar per week for fifty-two weeks or one cent the first week and an amount each week for the next fifty-one weeks that is double the previous week's amount. Which of the two should the sons choose?

Before saying which option the sons should choose, let us examine the two kinds of growth. The first kind of growth is linear, which demonstrates the principle of addition. In this kind of growth, there is an increase by a constant amount at regular time intervals. An unchanging amount is added at each of the regular time intervals. For example, a child grows one inch each year, or a miser hides ten dollars under a mattress each year. An unchanging amount (one inch or ten dollars) is added at regular intervals (once each year). The amount of increase each year is obviously not affected by the size of the child or the amount of money already under the mattress.

The other kind of growth is exponential growth, which demonstrates the principle of multiplication. In this kind of growth, there is an increase by a constant *percentage* of the whole at regular intervals. The amount added each time is *not* constant. The amount added increases continually as the total accumulated amount increases. An example of this kind of growth would be a colony of yeast cells that doubles every ten minutes. After ten minutes, one becomes two; after twenty minutes, two become four; and after thirty minutes, four become eight. The key to exponential growth is that the amount added increases each time.

Which of the two kinds of growth results in the greater growth in the long run? If you picked exponential growth, you were correct. With that in mind, which of the two options should the sons choose? They should choose the second option. If one is given one dollar each week, the last week he would still receive just one dollar, and his total accumulated amount would be fifty-two dollars.

The second choice is exponential, or multiplication. If one son chooses this, at the end of the year he will have an unbelievable amount of money. In fact, this boy's allowance in the last week—not the total amount accumulated over fifty-two weeks, but just his allowance for the fifty-second week—would be

$22,517,998,136,852.48. That is 22 trillion, 517 billion, 998 million, 136 thousand, 852 dollars and 48 cents. Initially, the multiplication is slow, but do not let that deceive you. In the long run, addition never keeps pace with multiplication. Multiplication is explosive.

Let's look at other examples. Suppose you start with a piece of paper 1/1000 of an inch thick, tear it in half, and then stack the halves, one on top of the other. At the end of one tearing, the thickness of the stack would be 2/1000 inch. If the process is repeated, the thickness would be 4/1000 inch. How high would the stack of paper be if it is torn just 50 times? Take a guess before reading on. The stack of paper, if it could be torn 50 times would be approximately 17,000,000 miles high. That equals 34 round trips to the moon.[9]

Or suppose one starts with a checkerboard of sixty-four squares. On the first square is placed one grain of wheat. On the second square are placed two grains, and on the third square are placed four grains. How much wheat would it take to complete the checkerboard if the number of grains is doubled on each succeeding square? It would take enough wheat to cover India to a depth of fifty feet.[10] The multiplication process is indeed explosive!

What is the point of all this? A discipling ministry must be built on exponential growth. Let's examine how the principle of multiplication relates to evangelism and the ministry of discipling others. Suppose an evangelist sees 1,000 people become believers every day.[11] At the end of the first year, there would be 365,000 new believers. That is the principle of addition—1,000 added every day.

Suppose another person in one year leads one person to Christ and spent that year building, teaching, and training that individual to grow to maturity and to give witness of his faith and build up others. At the end of the first year, those engaged in a discipling ministry would number two.

During the second year, the evangelist continues to lead 1,000 to Christ each day, making his total 730,000 people after

9. *The Navigators Association Discipleship Seminar Manual*, The Navigators, P.O. Box 20, Colorado Springs, CO 80901.
10. Henrichsen, p. 143.
11. Ibid., pp. 141-42.

two years. During that second year, the 2 people engaged in a discipling ministry go out and lead not 1,000 per day to Christ, but only 1 person each for the entire year. Time is spent with those individuals until, at the end of the year, they are able to spiritually reproduce themselves. Therefore, at the end of the second year, the disciples now total 4. If this process were to continue indefinitely, with the evangelist "adding" and the discipler "multiplying" each year, the total numbers of converts when compared later would reveal the following:

Years	Evangelist	Discipler
1	365,000	2
2	730,000	4
10	3,650,000	1,024
19	6,935,000	524,288
20	7,300,000	1,048,576
25	9,125,000	33,554,432
26	9,490,000	67,108,864
27	9,855,000	134,217,728
184	67,160,000	

It is very easy to see that, initially, the process of multiplication in discipling others is slower than the process of addition. In fact, 19 years would have to elapse before the number of those involved in a discipling ministry would exceed the evangelist's numbers of the first year alone. However, when the discipler reaches year 26, he has had a part in the winning of a total number of people that the evangelist will not reach for another 158 years. In other words, the number reached by the discipler by year 26 is not reached by the evangelist until year 184. In addition to all this, we do not have just converts in the discipling column but rather individuals who are built up in Christ and able to reproduce themselves spiritually. Men who are able to multiply themselves spiritually are a powerful force.

When could the numbers we just mentioned result in the winning of the entire world's population? Not taking into account population growth, and thus imagining the population to remain at 4 billion, the discipler could reach the world in 32 years. The evangelist would reach the world 10,960 years from now!

Now think of your group of Christians. Imagine what would happen if five of you or ten of you, or maybe twenty or thirty or fifty of you, began to win one person apiece to Christ, build that one up in the faith, and equip him to reproduce himself within a two-year period of time. What an impact that could have on your fellowship! I taught this material to a few people at a church where I was an associate pastor. Because I was the leader of the study, I wanted everyone's life in the study group to be cared for. I desired spiritual maturity in each person's life, so I began a discipling ministry. Things began rather slowly, but two years after we began, practically all of the people at the study were involved in discipling ministries, either as disciplers or disciples. Once the process has begun, it cannot help but grow.

But what are the marks of someone who is a multiplier? There are three essential characteristics, or marks.

MARK 1: TRAINED IN EVANGELISM

For someone to be able to reproduce himself, he needs to know how to lead an unbeliever to Christ. Phase 1 of discipling others is evangelism, and that is where a discipler begins his reproductive ministry.

MARK 2: TRAINED IN GROUNDING NEW CHRISTIANS IN THE FAITH

The discipler needs to know how to ground the new believer in the Christian walk. He needs to know what content is vital for a new Christian and what is necessary to bring that new Christian to maturity.

MARK 3: TRAINED IN EQUIPPING MATURE CHRISTIANS TO REPRODUCE THEMSELVES

Once an individual has been won to Christ and built up in Him, the discipler is to equip that mature Christian to conduct his own discipling ministry. In other words, a multiplier is able to help his disciple reproduce himself spiritually in someone else.

Of what do these three marks remind us? They remind us of three phases of a discipling ministry. A multiplier is one trained in each of the three phases discussed in chapter 2. The purpose of this book is to help you to become equipped in phase 3, that is, spiritual reproduction. This book is written in the hope that it will motivate you to reproduce your spiritual life in someone else.

4

DISCIPLING IN A WORD—
EXAMPLE

The value, definition, and goals of a discipling ministry are clear, but where do you begin? How do you get your disciples to those goals? Let's check our definition of discipling others:

Discipling others is the process
by which a Christian with a
life worth emulating
commits himself
for an extended period of time
to a few individuals
who have been
won to Christ, the
purpose being to aid
and guide their
growth to maturity and equip them to
reproduce themselves in a third spiritual generation.

Discipling others, as the last line of the definition states, is concerned with the third generation. But discipling takes place in the third generation only if something significant occurs in the second generation. And what takes place in the second generation is determined by whether anything significant is happening in you, the discipler. That is why our definition points to the idea of a "life worth emulating." That is where a discipling ministry begins—with the life-style of the discipler. And that is why your example is crucial. Therefore, one of your primary responsibilities as a discipler is to set a godly example. You must teach and live the truth, expound and exemplify the truth, talk and walk the truth, explain and exhibit the truth, lead by precept and practice, lead by lip and life. The spiritual principles you want lived out in your disciple's life must first be practiced by you.

SCRIPTURE

It is impossible to read the Bible without seeing the emphasis it places on example. Paul told the Corinthians that because he was their spiritual father, they were to be imitators (*mimētai*), or mimics, of him (1 Corinthians 4:16). They were also to be imitators of him in his example of not being a stumbling block to others (1 Corinthians 11:1). He told the Thessalonians that after they had become imitators (*mimētai*) of himself, Silvanus, and Timothy, they became examples (*tupon*), or a pattern to other believers (1 Thessalonians 1:6-7). Paul exhorted the Thessalonians to follow his example (*mimeisthai*) of a disciplined life, because he had offered himself as a model (*tupon*) for them to follow (2 Thessalonians 3:7, 9). Paul told Timothy to show himself as an example (*tupos*) of those who believe (1 Timothy 4:12) and to pay close attention to himself and his teaching, that is, his life and words (1 Timothy 4:16). Paul told Titus to be an example (*tupon*) of good deeds (Titus 2:6-8), and he exhorted the Philippians to follow his example (*tupon*; Philippians 3:17; see also 4:9). Peter told the elders to be examples (*tupoi*) to the flock (1 Peter 5:2-3). Thus throughout the New Testament we see the emphasis that is placed on being an example.

THE VALUE OF EXAMPLE

We know that discipling is based on the principle of example, but what exactly is the value of an example? Let's look at five ways in which a godly example is valuable.

VALUE 1: AN EXAMPLE IS A POWERFUL AGENT OF CHANGE

To encourage change, the life of a person is far more important than his words. It is not so much instruction that causes change as it is one's example.

We acquire new patterns of behavior by watching the example of others. Animals acquire new behavioral patterns in the same way. In one experiment, a monkey was placed in a situation in which she could observe the behavior of a woman. Here are the interesting results:

> At about 16 months of age she began to imitate such bits of household routine as dusting furniture and washing clothes and

dishes. Her early efforts were quite crude and could perhaps be ascribed to stimulus enhancement. Before she was two years old, however, some of her play was much too complex and precise to be so explained. For instance, she appropriated a lipstick, stood on the washbasin, looked in the mirror, and applied the cosmetic—not at random, but to her mouth. She then pressed her lips together and smoothed the color with her finger, just as she had seen the act performed. A similar performance occurred involving face powder.[1]

What a powerful effect an example has. You see it in little girls who play with their dolls. Usually the way they treat their dolls is the way their mothers have treated them. Remember the old television commercial? It was connected with the campaign to get people to stop smoking. The commercial showed a father and son who were walking together, and everything the father did, the son imitated.

The same effect is seen in a discipling relationship. To the young Christian a godly life is somewhat foreign. As an unbeliever, he had many ungodly models to observe. And they certainly had an effect on his life. But now, as a member of God's family, it is essential that he have at least one godly model. A discipler provides that for him. Think of the effect that older, mature Christians have had on your life. Are you able to be that kind of example to a young Christian?

VALUE 2: WE SEE THE CHRISTIAN LIFE IS POSSIBLE
WHEN WE SEE IT LIVED BY OTHERS

I will never forget the impact a young woman had in my early Christian life. She had a fervent love for people and the Lord. Often I would think, *Lord Jesus, I know the Christian life is really possible because I see it lived out in her.* Sometimes we get discouraged, grow weary, and lose heart in the battle. We wonder if there is any hope that we will mature. At such times we need to think of those who have gone before us, setting the example in consistency of walk and steadfastness. There are probably several people that you know whose lives have been a

1. K. J. Hayes and Catherine Hayes, "Imitation in a Home-raised Chimpanzee," *Journal of Comparative and Physiological Psychology* 45, no. 5 (October 1952): 451.

motivation and encouragement to you, just as your life will be a motivation to your disciple.

VALUE 3: WE LEARN TO FOLLOW THE LORD BY FOLLOWING THE LORD'S PEOPLE

Many times I am in tough situations, and I often think *I wonder what such and such a person would do?* God has given us godly examples. One man's strength might be evangelism, another's might be teaching, and another's might be wisdom in practical matters. These godly men simply become visible expressions and patterns of living from the invisible God I am trying to model. Some say, "Don't follow men; follow God. Keep your eyes on Christ." It is true that we are to follow only Christ and His pattern for living, but Christ's pattern for living is found in many individuals. Therefore, one way to follow God is to follow somebody else through whom God is walking. You will become that visible expression of the invisible God to the one you disciple.

VALUE 4: BEING THE RIGHT EXAMPLE GIVES YOU CREDIBILITY, ESPECIALLY WITH THOSE YOU DISCIPLE

Our lives are open exhibits. They will either prove or invalidate our spoken words. The way we live before others will determine our credibility. Paul's exhortation to Timothy in 1 Timothy 4:12 clearly expresses this point. Paul wrote, "Let no one look down on your youthfulness, but rather in speech, conduct, love, faith and purity, show yourself an example of those who believe." Timothy, who at that time was about thirty-five years old, was to gain the respect of those older than he through the living of a godly life. Being respected was not to be secured by reminding others of the position he had, that of apostolic representative. Neither was it to be secured by ordering people around. Timothy was to be an example in five areas of behavior. Through the living out of his life, he was to become credible and respected.

What about you? Do people respect you? Are you credible before others?

VALUE 5: SEEING THE EXAMPLES OF OTHERS ENCOURAGES
US TO ENGAGE IN ACTIVITIES THAT WE FORMERLY
FOUND THREATENING

I am sure there are certain actions that you are afraid to
take. But what would happen if you saw the success of someone
else in that particular action you fear? Your fear would probably
be greatly reduced. The Philippians were good examples of this.
Some of them became fearful when it came to telling others
about their faith. But the example of Paul's boldness in talking
to others about Christ encouraged the Philippians to testify with
courage. An action that was formerly thought threatening and
whose prospect inspired fear was undertaken as the result of the
example of an individual.

The one you disciple, because of your example, will be
encouraged to engage in activities that he used to find threatening.

EXAMPLE AND YOUR RESPONSIBILITY

We can all agree that being an example is quite a responsibility. Much of the direction Christendom takes in the future will
be determined by the models today's Christians follow. If the
models are unworthy of the name of Christ, then the Body of
Christ will suffer. It is imperative, therefore, that you be a
model who is worthy of being followed by new believers. Until
those you disciple are able to follow the Lord directly, you are
their picture of what Christ and the Christian life are like. What
you are will be reproduced in them.

This is the sobering aspect of example: they will reproduce
not only your strengths, but also your weaknesses. They will take
on your perspectives, convictions, strengths, and weaknesses.
Remember when Abraham lied to the people of Gerar, telling
them that Sarah was his sister (Genesis 20:1-7)? Do you know
who followed that pattern of behavior? Abraham's son Isaac did.
He did the very same thing in the same city (Genesis 26:1-11).

A most insightful verse on the effect of the discipler's example is Luke 6:40: "A pupil is not above his teacher; but everyone,
after he has been fully trained, will know as much as his teacher."
Is that what the verse says? No. A disciple will be "like" his
teacher. Those you disciple will be like you and will follow your
life-style, just as children follow their parents. One man has said

that he can see so much of himself in his children that they are like mirrors to him; he has four little mirrors walking around.

What is the key word in being an example? It is this—integrity. You are what you say. If a disciple continually sees a difference between what you say and what you do, you have lost your integrity.

Look at the life of Jesus. He always did what He told others to do. In Matthew 10, Jesus summoned the twelve disciples, instructed them, and then sent them out to preach the gospel. And when they were gone, what did Jesus do? "And it came about that when Jesus had finished giving instructions to His twelve disciples, He departed from there to teach and preach in their cities" (Matthew 11:1). He did exactly what He had told them to do. There was never a difference between what Christ said and what He did. He was always out in front, leading the way, demonstrating by example, and living the life He taught.

What about you? Are you living a life that others want to emulate? It is interesting that the Greek root word translated "example" and "model" in Philippians 3:17, 2 Thessalonians 3:9, 1 Timothy 4:12, and Titus 2:7 is *tupos*, which means "a pattern." People would lay down such a pattern and then trace over it.

Let me ask you a question. Can you ask people to trace their lives over yours? The fact is that you will reproduce yourself, whether you like it or not. The question is, What are you reproducing now? Let's suppose a new Christian were to be with you the whole day. What conclusions would he make concerning the Christian life based on what he saw of you that day?

I would like you to evaluate your life right now. Remember Luke 6:40? A disciple, after he has been fully trained, will be like the teacher, or discipler. If that is true—that those you disciple will become like you and those I disciple will become like me—what will that disciple be like? Write down the strengths and weaknesses that the disciple will have, based on your life-style. Consider the areas of attitudes, values, behavior, and habits.

Strengths	Weaknesses
1.	1.
2.	2.
3.	3.
4.	4.
5.	5.
6.	6.
7.	7.
8.	8.

Now close in prayer, thanking God for the strengths He has developed in your life and asking Him to begin dealing with your weaknesses.

Now that you have been faced with the importance of being an example, in the next chapter we will examine closely the kind of example you should be.

5

MARKS OF A DISCIPLER

In 1 Thessalonians 2:8, Paul gave us an insight into the nature of the discipling ministry. "Having thus a fond affection for you," he wrote, "we were well-pleased to impart to you not only the gospel of God but also *our own lives,* because you had become very dear to us" (emphasis added). Discipling someone is not a listing of steps to follow. It is not simply the transference of information but rather the imparting of one's life to another.

Therefore, in this chapter we want to look at the marks of a discipler who has a life worth imparting. Some of the marks will be encouraging to you; some, I hope, will be most convicting. At some points you may say, "I can never become a discipler if this is what is expected of me." That is a common attitude. But realize that you are progressing as a Christian. You are not fully mature. I am sure all of the marks are not lived out in your life in a perfect way, although they should be present to some degree. Nevertheless, the marks we will consider are the biblical standards. The Bible never caters to man's sinfulness or imperfections. It states exactly what the godly requirements are, the ideals, and you allow the Word to show you where you fall short. Then you let the Word train you to live righteously. So do not get discouraged. Remember, we are all in the process of growing. View the next few pages as a challenge and motivation in your walk with Christ.

COMMITMENT TO LOVING THE LORD JESUS CHRIST

One of the primary requirements for being a discipler is to love the Lord Jesus Christ. Why is that essential? The answer is found in Christ's encounter with Peter in John 21. We note that it was Jesus' desire that Peter serve the flock. In verse 15 He tells

Peter, "Tend My lambs." In verse 16 He says, "Shepherd My sheep." But interwoven in those verses was Christ's desire to confirm in Peter's mind the fact of Peter's love for Him. Jesus did not ask Peter, "Peter, do you love the flock?" No! Christ said, "Do you love Me?" Jesus knew that if He could establish Peter's love for Himself, then Peter would not have any problems in caring for the Lord's people.

But what does it mean to love the Lord Jesus? First of all, love for Christ manifests itself in *obedience*. In John 21:19, Jesus tells Peter, "Follow Me." The biblical idea of what it means to love Christ is to obey Him. John 14:15 says, "If you love Me, you will keep My commandments." Therefore, if you want to know whether you are loving Christ, do not ask yourself, "'How many times have I told the Lord, 'I love You'?" That is not the measure of love at all. Words mean nothing. Your love certainly is not determined by how emotional you become when talking of the Lord. The issue when measuring your love for Him is the degree of your obedience. Are you obedient to Christ? Loving Christ is not an emotion but rather is a matter of obedience.

Second, loving Christ means that you must nurture your love-walk with Him. This nurturing means spending time with Him, getting to know His love for you, and communicating with Him. Such love means having a vital, personal relationship with Him, and unless you have that kind of relationship with Christ, you have nothing to say to your disciples.

A discipler who does not have a love-walk with Christ cannot lead his disciple to walk with Christ. When I was on the staff of a Christian organization, I would spend six to eight hours a day on a campus, meeting with Christians and talking to unbelievers. At those times when I failed to cultivate my walk with the Lord, my conscience naturally began to accuse me. It had good reason. Going on campus and trying to exhort others to live a godly life when I was not nurturing my own love-walk with Christ was like trying to run the marathon without any preparation. I would lose all confidence in doing or saying anything. It was very difficult for my mouth to be exhorting someone to love Christ with all his strength when my heart was not rejoicing in Him.

What is the problem in such a situation? It is not so much out-and-out sin as much as it is neglect—neglecting to worship

Him, neglecting to relate my life to Him, neglecting to talk to Him, and neglecting to be honest with Him.

Unless you cultivate a love-walk with Christ, you will have nothing to say to the one you disciple. Ask yourself: What should I begin to incorporate into my life-style (both attitudes and actions) that will improve my love-walk with the Lord Jesus Christ?

HEART FOR PEOPLE

Read the following verses carefully:

For *I long to see you* in order that I may impart some spiritual gift to you, that you may be established. (Romans 1:11, emphasis added)

For it is only right for me to feel this way about you all, because *I have you in my heart.* (Philippians 1:7, emphasis added)

For God is my witness, how *I long for you all* with the affection of Christ Jesus. (Philippians 1:8, emphasis added)

Yet to remain on in the flesh is more necessary for your sake. And convinced of this, I know that I shall remain and continue with you *all for your progress and joy in the faith.* (Philippians 1:24-25, emphasis added)

[concerning Timothy] For I have no one else of kindred spirit who will genuinely *be concerned for your welfare.* (Philippians 2:20, emphasis added)

Therefore, my *beloved brethren whom I long to see.* (Philippians 4:1, emphasis added)

[concerning Epaphras] For I bear him witness that he has a *deep concern for you* and for those who are in Laodicea and Hierapolis. (Colossians 4:13, emphasis added)

What are these verses saying? They are saying that we are to be lovers of people. It would be foolish for a person without this love to commit himself to a discipling ministry, because he will not last in such a ministry.

What is involved in the biblical principle of loving people? John 13:1 states that Jesus, "having loved His own who were in the world, He loved them to the end." But how did He love them? Verses four and five of John 13 tell us that Jesus "rose from supper, and laid aside His garments; and taking a towel, girded Himself about. Then He poured water into the basin, and began to wash the disciples' feet, and to wipe them with the towel with which He was girded." Jesus' love was expressed by a commitment to serve them. As we saw in the first mark of a discipler, loving Jesus, we tend to connect the idea of love with a feeling. But love is not an emotion. It is an act of commitment. When we love God, it is a commitment to obey. When we love people, it is a commitment to serve.

When we love with a commitment to serve, the feelings of love follow. There have been some men that I have discipled toward whom I had no particular feelings in the early stages of meeting with them. I would see them regularly, but my thoughts at times were not, *Oh boy! Another chance to meet my disciple. What a thrill! What a joy!* My feelings toward meeting them were not always exciting and thrilling, and yet I was committed to them. I desired to serve them and see them become successful in the Christian life. I was committed to doing all that God expected me to do in helping them become men of God. And an amazing thing happened after a period of time. The feelings began to come. A deep sense of personal joy would flood me, and that personal joy would result in greater commitment to them on my part, which would in turn result in their becoming an even greater blessing and joy to me. Commitment to people is the key, with the feelings of love following.

Here is another question to ask yourself: What problems do I have with people that will prevent me from loving them? Maybe it is hard for you to be committed to others of a certain race or ethnic or socioeconomic background. Possibly there are people with a certain kind of personality that you find difficult to love.

I often think about the men Jesus discipled. How different they were. Simon the Zealot and Matthew were at extremes. Peter was an "up front" man. Andrew seemed to like the background. Can you imagine Jesus choosing the twelve this way: "Let's see now. You fit into the mold of the kind of person I could love, so follow Me. Your kind of personality would clash with Mine, so I do not think it would be wise for you to follow Me." Jesus simply loved, and if others got in the way, they, too, were loved.

Is your love for people like Christ's? What if you led someone to Christ who had habits you could not stand or a personality different from your own? Do you have a love for people, a commitment to serve them, that is able to overcome any possible barrier?

HOLY, GODLY LIFE

God has always used pure instruments. In fact, your usefulness to God as a discipler is in direct proportion to your purity. God does not primarily use men with great ideas or great intellect, but rather men with great likeness to Jesus Christ. Second Timothy 2:21 speaks to this: "Therefore, if a man cleanses himself from these things [the "things" of verses 14-20], he will be a vessel for honor, sanctified, useful to the Master, prepared for every good work." What is the principle? Cleansing precedes usefulness. That only makes sense when talking about serving a holy God. Would Van Cliburn use an out-of-tune piano? Would Johnny Bench have used a cracked bat? Would Rembrandt have used a dirty brush? Obviously not. Could we then expect a holy God to use anything but people who are holy? One often wonders at the secret of Paul's ministry. Why did he have such an impact? First Thessalonians 2:10 gives us the answer: "You are witnesses, and so is God, how devoutly and uprightly and blamelessly we behaved toward you believers." Is it any wonder that Paul had such a dynamic ministry? God uses holy, cleansed vessels. Paul realized that. He exhorts Timothy in 1 Timothy 4:16 to "pay close attention to yourself."

What is holiness? A holy person is not a perfect person but a progressing person. To be fit for God's use does not mean that you are perfect but that you are dealing with sin. That is what allows you to be an example even though you sin. It is not the absence of sin that makes you an example. Rather, it is knowing how to answer to imperfection and sin in a godly manner. What is that manner? Confession. First John 1:9 states that a characteristic of a Christian is that he is a confessor of sins. In other words, he agrees with God that he has sinned, and then he repents. He stops committing the sin. Look at Ezra 10:11: "Make confession to the LORD God of your fathers, and do His will." There you have the two parts of getting right with God after your sin—confession and repentance.

The exciting thing is that we do not have to live one minute of our lives without the joy of fellowship with our God. One I discipled once said to me, "Allen, I'm getting to the point that when I recognize sin in my life, I just want to deal with it right then and there." That is the right attitude!

There simply is no way that you can be effective as a discipler unless you are dealing with your sins. Unconfessed sin saps all the power. It is very hard to fake peace, joy, and freedom from guilt. It is very hard to exhort someone to holy living when personal, unconfessed sin is staring you in the face. We each need to come to the point at which our desire for holiness is greater than our desire to serve God in any ministry, especially a discipling ministry.

Ask yourself: What areas of my life do I tend to try to hide from God, in the process keeping myself from being honest and open with Him? Can you think of any right now? Why not pray and tell God of your desire to be cleansed. Make David's request yours:

> Search me, O God, and know my heart;
> Try me and know my anxious thoughts;
> And see if there be any hurtful way in me,
> And lead me in the everlasting way.
>
> (Psalm 139:23-24)

PURE MOTIVES

Why do you want to be involved in discipling others? What are your reasons? There are many wrong motives. For example, some people disciple because such a ministry fulfills needs in their lives. What would a person like that do once the discipling ministry no longer met his needs? Would he slowly withdraw from the discipling relationships he had begun? That motive is obviously selfish. Others disciple because of a "have to" spirit. They have been intimidated by other Christians who have made them think that unless they got involved in a discipling ministry, God would no longer accept them. Others disciple because they desire to have power over others. Discipling is to them a means of lording it over people. These are just a few of the many wrong motives one can have in desiring a discipling ministry.

But what are proper motivations for engaging in a discipling ministry? Ultimately, the only reason to do anything is that God will be glorified. "Whether, then, you eat or drink, or whatever you do, do all to the glory of God" (1 Corinthians 10:31). One way to glorify God is to produce people whose lives display the character of Christ. That was Paul's desire. His motive for his ministry was the spiritual welfare of others, whose lives would then be glorifying to God. For evidence of this motive, look at 1 Thessalonians 2:11-12:

> Just as you know how we were exhorting and encouraging and imploring each one of you as a father would his own children, *so that you may walk in a manner worthy of the God who calls you into His own kingdom and glory.* (Emphasis added)

A desire to produce people whose walk was worthy of God—that was Paul's motive for getting involved in people's lives. In Colossians 1:28-29, also, Paul says that it was for a specific purpose that he labored. What was the purpose? "[To] present every man complete in Christ" (v. 28). The desire to see spiritual growth and maturity in others was Paul's motive in his ministry. His concern was completely for the spiritual welfare of others. He knew that mature Christian lives would ultimately bring glory to God.

Ask yourself: What changes must I make in my motives for discipling others if I am to be a God-pleasing discipler? Are you considering a discipling ministry because of some selfish need it would meet in your life? Or are your motives concern for the welfare of others and a desire that God be glorified? Before reading on, take some time to talk to God concerning your motives.

FULL UNDERSTANDING OF THE DEMANDS OF DISCIPLING OTHERS

To fully understand the demands on a discipler is most sobering to those interested in a discipling ministry. The demands can be reduced to two words, sacrifice and cost. Discipling someone, because of the demands placed on the discipler, will mean times of personal sacrifice. And indeed, whenever one becomes a servant of others, there is a cost. The discipler will have to give up many of his own rights and desires. Does that appeal to you?

Discipling means hard work. Jesus realized that when He commissioned the disciples in Matthew 28:18-20. We often take the last line of verse 20 out of context and apply it to God's presence being with us wherever we are. Of course that is true—God is always with us—but the primary meaning of that verse is that when you are engaged in the work of winning men to Christ and building them up in the faith, Christ promises to be with you, strengthening you, encouraging you, and enabling you. Christ realized that the task would not be easy and that many of us would give up, so He spoke to our need for His presence.

This idea of God's presence with His servants is not unique to the Great-Commission passage. Whenever God knew that a certain task would be difficult or place many demands on His people, He promised His presence. For example, God promised His presence to Moses, who was afraid to approach Pharaoh (Exodus 3:12); to Joshua before entering the Promised Land (Joshua 1:5); and to Gideon, who had the task of delivering Israel from the Midianites (Judges 6:16). Do you get the point? God's presence is promised when His people engage themselves in tasks for Him that are demanding and difficult.

Paul realized the hard work that involvement in people's lives entails. He says in Colossians 1:28-29 that he labored to present every man complete in Christ. In other words, Paul toiled to the point of exhaustion. He says the same thing to the Thessalonians, in 1 Thessalonians 2:9: "For you recall, brethren, our labor and hardship, how working night and day so as not to be a burden to any of you, we proclaimed to you the gospel of God."

What about the context of 2 Timothy 2:2? We all know what 2 Timothy 2:2 says, but do you know what verses 3 through 6 say? Verse 2 says to pass the baton to future generations, but verses 3 through 6 describe what will be required of you as you pass the baton. You are to be like a suffering soldier who makes a personal sacrifice, a competing athlete who is disciplined, and a hard-working farmer who perseveres and is tenacious. You should not be committed to verse 2 unless you are equally committed to living out verses 3 through 6.

Because they are so great, you need to understand the demands that a discipling ministry will place upon your life.

Discipling others is not the kind of ministry you blindly walk into, so let's look at six demands that are made of a discipler. Tom Kehn's unpublished thesis, has been helpful to me in this area.

1. TIME

There is no escaping the demand on the discipler's time. The discipling ministry asks you to sacrifice your time in two ways, long range and day by day. The sacrifice is long range because once you see the importance of a discipling ministry and commit yourself to it, you are in effect saying no to many other activities and commitments. It is a day-by-day demand on time because some time that you want to spend on yourself may have to be sacrificed if it means meeting the needs of the disciple. Believe me, you are on twenty-four-hour call as a discipler.

2. EMOTIONAL STRENGTH

Kehn discusses the need for emotional strength:

Because of the fact that the ministry of discipleship is a long, enduring responsibility with personal involvement, it may well drain the person emotionally, Discipleship requires patience, understanding, and compassion. The discipler should be so involved in the person's life that he shares his burdens in a real way. Christ, in dealing with people, was moved with empathy to the point of tears. The discipler should feel this type of empathy for his maturing friend.[1]

Kehn's statement sounds much like Paul in 2 Corinthians 11:29. "Who is weak without my being weak? Who is led into sin without my intense concern?" Paul said. Or read the book of 1 Corinthians. Don't you think that dealing with the Corinthians' sins drained Paul emotionally? Or what about those men who were persecuting the Thessalonians? The Thessalonians were so precious to Paul, and he was deeply concerned. In fact, he was so deeply concerned that when he "could endure it no longer,"

1. Thomas Kehn, "The Ministry of Youth Discipleship: Its Questions and Answers," Master's thesis, Talbot Theological Seminary, 1975, pp. 57-58.

he sent Timothy to find out about their faith (1 Thessalonians 3:5). Paul got involved with people, and you can be sure that he had to deal repeatedly with his emotions.

Often I have been emotionally drained by praying for the men I have discipled, especially when they were going through intense struggles. Sometimes I would wake up in the middle of the night, thinking about them and their needs. Even though you cast the disciples' burdens on the Lord, you still feel the weight of their burdens to some extent. Discipling is indeed costly.

3. PHYSICAL STRENGTH

There will be times in your discipling ministry when you will be asked to make physical sacrifices for the sake of the disciple. There will be times when you will be physically tired and in need of rest, and you will receive a phone call from a discouraged brother or sister who needs your help. There will be times when you will be hungry and sitting at the table with your family, when there will be a knock on the door. After two hours of counseling the disciple, you may be able to eat. That is what is involved in a discipling ministry. One night I heard a knock on the door at 4:00 A.M. It was a young man I was discipling who was in need. Being available to meet needs means being accessible *whenever* the needs arise. Hurts and trials do not come only between nine and five.

One passage in the gospel narratives fascinates me because it reveals Christ's unbelievable willingness to submit to physical demands if it meant the welfare of the disciples. The passage describes Christ's "longest day," and it begins in Matthew 12. We see Him being accused by the Pharisees of breaking the Sabbath. We see Him healing people, and we see Him discussing the blasphemy of the Holy Spirit. We see Him answering the scribes and Pharisees who asked Him for a sign. We see Him dealing with His mother and brothers, who were seeking Him. We see Him in chapter 13 (which describes events of the same day) teaching the parables of the kingdom. Finally in Mark 4, a parallel chapter, we see Him at the end of a long day, sleeping in a boat, totally exhausted. But the day did not end there. Wind and waves were tossing the boat so much that it was filling with water. The frightened disciples awakened Him. It is said of Jesus in verse 39, "And being aroused, He rebuked the disciples and said to them, 'Can't you see that I'm trying to get some sleep! It has been a long day!' " Is that what it says? No. That is probably what I would have said. But Christ rebuked the wind, not the disciples, and then calmed the sea. even though He was physically exhausted, He still met their needs. What an example Christ is to us!

4. FINANCIAL AND MATERIAL POSSESSIONS

As the new Christian walks with Christ, many things that can stimulate his growth become available to him in the form of Christian tape recordings, conferences, and books. There will be times when the discipler, because of the disciple's lack of money, will think it is important to provide the money that is needed. For the sake of the disciple's growth and benefit, you, as the discipler, must be willing to make the necessary sacrifices.

5. LACK OF PUBLIC RECOGNITION

Is it public recognition that you are after? If so, the discipling ministry is not for you. It does not have the prestige or glamour that other kinds of ministry have. If you are seeking the approval, applause, and recognition of others, you are not ready to begin a discipling relationship. Few people will see you labor in discipling the individual whom God has entrusted to your care. They will not notice the hours you spend teaching the disciples, counseling them in their problems, and praying for them. There is no public recognition—just a deep, personal sense of satisfaction and fulfillment in seeing lives changed right before your eyes. What more do you need?

6. EXPOSURE TO PERSONAL INADEQUACIES AND WEAKNESSES

In chapter 1, we saw that one of the by-products of a discipling ministry is the purification that takes place in the discipler's own life. As you disciple others, you are continually exposed to areas of weakness in your life. Your inadequacies surface very fast. You learn very quickly that there are no six-million-dollar "bionic" disciplers. Unless you allow yourself to make mistakes and fail in the discipling ministry, the temptation will be to give up. You need to have the courage to stand strong, even when confronted with your own inadequacies and weaknesses.

Ask yourself: What demands made of me by the discipling ministry are most difficult for me to handle?

CONSISTENCY IN WITNESSING TO OTHERS

In the chapter entitled "The Definition of Discipling" we noticed that the first phase of discipling others is evangelism. Reproduction cannot take place if there is no growth, and there can be no growth without birth. Yet even though this is true, most Christians do not know how to tell others of their faith in a clear, concise, and positive manner. It is imperative that every believer receive some kind of training in evangelism. There are so many tracts and programs available that there is no excuse for not knowing how to tell others about the Christian faith.

Ask yourself: What fears must I overcome, and what actions must I take, if I am to be a consistent witness for Christ? What are the fears you have in giving witness of your faith? Do you lack boldness? Do you lack training in how to tell others about Christ? Another fear that many have is that they lack a credible life to back up the claims of the gospel. Is that your fear? What about the consistency of your witness for Christ? When was the last time you gave witness of your faith to someone else? Do you tend to tell others about the gospel only in certain places, such as at work or school or in people's homes, and avoid other settings? Could you say that telling others about the gospel is a way of life with you? One thing that strikes me about Paul is that the gospel was always on his tongue, no matter where he was. In Acts 17:17 we see this most clearly: "So he was reasoning in the synagogue with the Jews and the God-fearing Gentiles, and in the market place every day *with those who happened to be present*" (emphasis added). Paul did not limit his proclaiming of God's good news to just those who were in the synagogue. He went to the place of worship *and* the place of business. He witnessed wherever he went, and if someone got in his way, that person, too, heard the message.

I would challenge you to make witnessing for Christ a way of life. Wherever you are, talk to people. I have developed transitional sentences that have helped me move conversations to spiritual thoughts. They have been most effective. After I have met someone and talked to him for a while, I will say: "Joe [or whatever his name might be], I was wondering if I could ask you a question? I am really interested in what people are thinking spiritually. Do you often think about God or Jesus?" Believe it or not, that approach has opened up conversations with a gas station attendant, a waitress at a restaurant, a butcher at a supermarket, a checker at a grocery store, and many others. All of them were willing to tell me their views, and then I had the opportunity to witness to them. Two young men to whom I witnessed in this way later became part of a discipling group that I was leading.

It is through evangelism that you produce disciples. Why not pray and tell God of your availability to witness for Him to others. Then when God is faithful in bringing people across your path, break the "sound barrier" and tell them the good news of the gospel.

UNDERSTANDING OF THE HOLY SPIRIT'S ROLE IN DISCIPLING OTHERS

Entering into a discipling ministry can be threatening at times because of the responsibility that is placed on you as a discipler. You are caring for someone for whom Christ died. That responsibility should not be taken lightly. Yet it is a comfort to know that the Holy Spirit is very influential in the process of discipling someone. His role touches two areas.[2]

1. The Holy Spirit causes growth in the believer. Knowing that the responsibility to produce spiritual growth in those I disciple does not ultimately rest on me lets me relax. It took me some time to realize that the major responsibility for the disciple's growth is not mine. I used to think that the human element, the discipler, has the major role in someone's growth, and

2. Ibid., pp. 66-69. I am indebted to Thomas Kehn for ideas in this section.

the Holy Spirit just helps out. But that is not the case. God causes the growth through the Holy Spirit (1 Corinthians 3:6). He is the One who convicts, encourages, and reveals truth. The Holy Spirit's role in causing growth certainly does not negate the responsibility of the discipler, however. Rather, they work together, the Holy Spirit as the source and the discipler as the instrument.

2. The Holy Spirit ministers to isolated believers. There will be times when the new Christian is isolated from the one who led him to Christ. That may be due to geographical separation, the discipler's failure to maintain contact, or the new Christian's simply wanting to be left alone. It is comforting to know that when you cannot be with the new Christian, you can rely on the Holy Spirit to cause him to grow in his walk with Christ. Of course, contact should be maintained through letters, phone calls, and visits whenever possible.

Ask yourself: How much of an emphasis do I place on the Holy Spirit's role in my discipling ministry? Do you really believe that the ultimate responsibility for growth lies in the Holy Spirit, or are you assuming the *entire* weight? Are you relying on the Holy Spirit to produce changes? Do you have a clear understanding of how the human and divine agents complement each other in a discipling ministry?

PERSON OF PRAYER

If you are like most Christians, you do not pray nearly as much as you should. Why is it that most Christians struggle with prayer? Could it be that we really do not believe it can get things done? Yet prayer should be the foundation of all that we do. It is especially important in a discipling ministry. I am often amazed at the effect my prayers have in the lives of those whom I disciple, yet at times praying is the last thing I do. I spend time exhorting, admonishing, encouraging, teaching, and counseling someone, using any angle I can to see change in his life, but nothing happens. And then I pray. You know the saying "When all else fails, pray." It really should be "Before anything fails, pray." After I pray, asking God to cause change in a person's life, I begin to see those specific changes. Those are the times in which I realize that discipling someone is a supernatural ministry.

Believe me, there will be times when your disciple needs to change in a specific area. What will be your first reaction? Will you first think through all the verses you want to show him? Will you recite in your mind how you will exhort him? Or will you first get on your knees and ask God to cause a change in his behavior? If you are not a person of prayer, I can guarantee that the discipling ministry will be frustrating.

Look at the emphasis the following verses put on prayer:

> I thank my God in all my remembrance of you, *always offering prayer* with joy in every prayer for you all, in view of your participation in the gospel from the first day until now. (Philippians 1:3-5, emphasis added)

> We give thanks to God always for all of you, *making mention of you in our prayers.* (1 Thessalonians 1:2, emphasis added)

> For what thanks can we render to God for you in return for all the joy with which we rejoice before our God on your account, *as we night and day keep praying* most earnestly that we may see your face, and may complete what is lacking in your faith? (1 Thessalonians 3:9-10, emphasis added)

Of course, we cannot overlook Jesus' ministry of prayer for His men. John 17 is filled with requests made by Jesus to His Father for His men. And what about Epaphras? What a model he is for any discipler to follow. Paul mentioned Epaphras in his letter to the Colossians:

> Epaphras, who is one of your number, a bondslave of Jesus Christ, sends you his greetings, *always laboring earnestly for you in his prayers*, that you may stand perfect and fully assured in all the will of God. (Colossians 4:12, emphasis added)

Epaphras toiled to the point of exhaustion in his prayers for the Colossians. Ask yourself, When was the last time I felt exhausted because of my prayers for those I am discipling? Do their needs grip me and drive me to my knees? Consider this: What must I do to make my prayer life more pleasing to God?

STUDENT OF THE BIBLE

You, as a discipler, must be a student of the Bible for two reasons. First, you must study the Word for your personal growth. How else can you cultivate your love-walk with Christ except by spending time in His Word? And second, you must study the Bible for the discipling ministry. Discipling involves teaching, counseling, comforting, and encouraging the disciple. Where do you go to learn principles of godly living to teaching the disciple? The Word. Where is wisdom found to counsel a disciple with a problem? The Word. Where do you go to comfort a sorrowing believer? The Word. Where is encouragement found for a Christian who is discouraged? The Word. Is it any wonder, then, that you, as a discipler, must be a diligent student of the Word?

When I meet with those I am discipling, they will usually have a question on some aspect of Christian living, or else they will be struggling with a specific problem. When they come to me with a question or problem, I have to make a decision. Will I use my own opinions in answering them, or will I take them to God's answers in the Word? If any lasting changes are to take place in the disciple's life, God's Word, not mine, has to be the basis of all answers. That is why one of the primary tasks of a discipler is to instill within the disciple submission to and respect for the Word of God. When that is established, changing the disciple is easy. Then when an issue arises, because there is an attitude of submission to the Word, finding the disciple's answer is simply a matter of the discipler's pointing out the biblical principles relating to the subject. Obedience to those biblical principles should then follow.

The need to be able to help the disciple find biblical principles makes it imperative that a discipler have a broad understanding of the Word. But what kind of knowledge is necessary? First, the discipler needs doctrinal knowledge. How do we know that Jesus is God? What was involved in the atonement? What does inspiration mean? There are many such elementary yet crucial questions. Second, the discipler needs basic Bible knowledge. Who wrote the books of the Bible? When and why were they written? You might even be asked who Leviticus was, or when Sodom and Gomorrah got married! Third, the discipler has to have practical knowledge. What does Scripture have to say about worry? guilt? doubt? finances? relationships? All three kinds of knowledge are necessary. Now, do not panic. Remember that you, as a discipler, are constantly learning and increasing in knowledge. The disciples may ask many questions for which you will not have answers. Great! That will motivate you to find the answers.

Ask yourself: What must I incorporate into my schedule if I am to be a student of the Bible?

MATURING, BALANCED GROWTH

Growth in the discipler's life is essential, and such growth takes on two forms. First, your growth is to be a maturing growth. In Philippians 3, Paul uses language that describes his own growth process. In verse 12 he says that he *presses on* to maturity. In verse 13 he forgets the past and *reaches forward* to what lies ahead for him. In verse 14 he again says that he *presses on* toward the goal. Paul knew nothing of Christian living that was stagnant, static, or neutral. He was constantly moving forward, trusting God for bigger things, and learning more about his Lord. In the midst of a discipling ministry, you must continue to grow in your walk with Christ? Why? You can only reproduce in your disciples what has been developed first in your own life. There needs to be in your life that which is reproducible. The simple fact is that you can only take someone else as far as you have gone yourself. You can never lead your disciples to growth beyond your own level of maturity. Once they reach your level of maturity, the guardian-example role ceases. The relationship then becomes a spiritual peer relationship with no leader or follower.

The second important idea relating to the discipler's growth in Christ is that it needs to be a balanced growth. This point haunts me. I know what my strengths are, and I am confident that the men I am discipling will develop those same strengths. But it is equally probable that they will develop my weaknesses. The same will be true in your discipling ministry. If the emphasis of your life is on the study of Scripture to the exclusion of other godly disciplines, it is safe to assume that that will be your disciple's emphasis. If you are exclusively committed to the task of evangelism, so will be your disciples. That is a most challenging thought. How we need to present a balanced view of the Christian life!

Ask yourself: What must I do if I am to have a maturing, balanced Christian life?

6

SELECTING AND CHALLENGING POTENTIAL DISCIPLES

Let's retrace our steps before we move into the topic of selecting and challenging potential disciples. We first looked at the value of discipling others and studied the relationship of discipling to Christ, the disciple, the discipler, the church, and the world. We next examined the definition and goals of discipling others and saw that the starting point for discipling others is to have a life worth emulating. Discipling others begins with the example of the discipler. We then looked at ten marks of a discipler. This chapter on selecting and challenging potential disciples takes us back to our definition of discipling others:

> Discipling others is the process
> by which a Christian with a
> life worth emulating
> commits himself
> for an extended period of time *to a few individuals*
> who have been
> won to Christ, the
> purpose being to
> aid and guide their
> growth to maturity and equip them to
> reproduce themselves in a third spiritual generation.

The sixth line of the definition states that the discipler commits himself to *a few individuals*. This is the part of the definition that we want to examine in this chapter. How does a person who desires to disciple someone go about finding that individual? How does he select and then challenge a person to be involved in a discipling relationship?

Before we discuss those questions, it should be pointed out that there are basically two formats in a discipling ministry. The

71

first format is the one-on-one relationship. This is the relationship in which just you and the disciple get together. No one else is involved. The "few individuals" mentioned in the definition could be one one-on-one relationship, two one-on-one relationships, or whatever number you want. The second format is the small group. This is the relationship in which you meet with a "few individuals" at one time in a small-group meeting. This book is geared more to the one-on-one approach than to the small group, although the small-group approach will be discussed. So when we talk about selecting and challenging disciples in this chapter, it will be with a view to challenging them to a one-on-one relationship as opposed to joining a small group.

SELECTING POTENTIAL DISCIPLES

NUMBER OF DISCIPLES

The question you will have as you begin a discipling ministry is this: *How many people should I disciple?* Although it is impossible for me to answer that for you, there are several points that you need to keep in mind as you make that determination. First, Jesus was concerned with quality, not quantity, in His discipling ministry. His goal was quantity in the sense that He wanted many people to believe in Him and be built up in Him, but the means of reaching the multitude (quantity) was the close relationship (quality) with a few. There is no question but that the deep level of commitment to the twelve paved the way for the masses to be reached. Because personal contact and time are essential elements in building a quality relationship, you must be careful not to try to disciple more people than you have the time to handle. As you think through your schedule, it may be that you can disciple only one person, or maybe three, or maybe seven. Whatever the number may be, work with them and go for quality. Waylon Moore in *New Testament Follow-up* has stated well the case for emphasizing quality:

A decision that our ministry will be intensive rather than extensive will change our whole life. Quality begets quantity. It takes vision to disciple a man to reach the mass. If you train one man then you penetrate the multitude.[1]

It is also important to understand your own limitations. You may be limited by experience. If you are just beginning a discipling ministry, it may be wise for you to disciple only one person. Pray that God would give you wisdom to know exactly the number of individuals you can disciple.

GOD-GIVEN PEOPLE

In Christ's prayer to His Father in John 17, He refers to the men God has given Him. "I manifested Thy name *to the men whom Thou gavest Me* out of the world; Thine they were and Thou gavest them to Me, and they have kept Thy word" (John 17:6; emphasis added). "I ask on their behalf; I do not ask on behalf of the world, but of *those whom Thou has given Me;* for they are Thine" (John 17:9; emphasis added). If Jesus commands us to go and make disciples, is it not reasonable to assume that He will send us people whom He wants us to lead to a saving knowledge of Himself and then help build up in Him? If He gives us a command, He will also give us that which we need to obey the command. I believe that God has people ready to be won and taught by you. Just as He gave certain men to the Lord Jesus, so He has individuals prepared to send your way.

ERROR OF HASTY SELECTION

As you examine Jesus' life, do you find that He was hasty in selecting His disciples? Absolutely not. He took His time, waiting for God to give Him the right individuals, and He certainly did not take everyone who came to Him. In fact, it appears that Jesus had an encounter with each of His disciples prior to His actually calling them to follow Him, an encounter that gave Him the chance to observe the potential disciple's reaction to His teaching. It will probably be true of you that the individuals you disciple will be people you already know. They might be people who have the same interests as yourself, although it is also true that if you lead someone to Christ, it is your responsibility to

1. Waylon B. Moore, *New Testament Follow-Up: For Pastors and Laymen* (Grand Rapids, Mich.: Eerdmans, 1963), p. 68.

look after the welfare of that person whether your interests are similar or not. Whoever the individual might be, do not jump quickly into a relationship with him. Something else is necessary before selecting the person—prayer.

PRAYER IN SELECTING

The decision to disciple someone is a most important decision. To disciple someone means a commitment of time and yourself, and the commitment should not be entered into lightly. Whom you select is crucial. Therefore, you need to pray and seek God's direction concerning that decision. In Luke 6 we see how important prayer was to Jesus as He selected His men. "And it was at this time that He went off to the mountain to pray, and.He spent the whole night in prayer to God. And when day came, He called His disciples to Him; and chose twelve of them, whom he also named as apostles" (Luke 6:12-13).

ROLE OF DISCIPLES' ABILITY IN YOUR DECISION

Christ's selection of His men was certainly not on the basis of their ability. He chose them not so much for what they were, but rather for what He knew they would become. One man has stated well Jesus' criteria in choosing disciples:

The men whom Jesus selected to be His disciples represented basically an average cross section of the population of His day. Their names were not found in the latest *Who's Who*, nor were they listed among the "top ten" in fashion, education, wealth, or "most likely to succeed." They were certainly not the type of individuals one would choose to revolutionize the world. Yet, these are exactly the types of individuals Jesus selected.

Christ did not choose disciples on the basis of ability. He was not looking for great personality, size or beauty. As is recorded in I Samuel 16:7, "man looketh on the outward appearance, but the Lord looketh on the heart." Jesus was looking for hearts totally available to Him. It did not take much of a man to be a disciple, but it took all of him that there was. . . . He had a keen eye for the character of an individual in the first place (e.g., Nathanael—John 1:47), and as keen an eye to discern what he had in him to become (e.g., John 1:42, "Thou art Simon—thou salt be called Cephas.") Jesus saw and selected men not only for what they were, but for what they were to become. He selected them for their potential. Men were His method, and He selected men with potentially keen and sensitive spiritual senses.[2]

The disciples' potential was foremost in Christ's mind, and that must be your perspective. You must not turn anyone down simply because he appears not to have the intelligence and ability to be a disciple of Christ. God is in the business of making each of His children into a significant person.

GENDER OF DISCIPLES

Discipling someone is a transference of life-style, which requires that much time be spent with the disciple. Discipling involves counseling the disciple when he has specific needs and problems. It demands honesty and openness between the discipler and disciple. It is an intense fellowship with a long-term commitment. Because of these aspects in the nature of a discipling relationship, it is obvious that there would be many limitations in discipling someone of the opposite sex. By all means, you are to minister to those of the opposite sex. All of the "one another" commands of Scripture (e.g., love one another, encourage one another) are to be applied to everyone in the Body of Christ. You certainly are not to avoid ministries to those of the opposite sex. But to begin discipling members of the opposite sex in the way I am using the term *discipling* would be very unwise. What happens, then, if you meet someone of the opposite sex who wants to grow in Christ and needs that personal attention? The best thing to do is to lead that person to someone of his (or her) own sex.

QUALITIES IN DISCIPLES

We discussed the principle that you are not to choose a disciple on the basis of what he is now but rather on the basis of what he can become. Do not look for ability, but potential. Yet even though you are looking for potential, there are certain qualities that you must look for in a person whom you desire to

2. Robert D. Sappington II, "A Manual for Discipling Teens," Master's thesis, Talbot Theological Seminary, 1974, pp. 34–35.

disciple. Unfortunately, looking for specific qualities can be somewhat subjective. How can you be sure that the individual truly exhibits all the characteristics to be described? To what degree must you see those qualities in his life before you select him? It is difficult to answer these questions, but let's now discuss some of the qualities you should look for.

Christian. The person you desire to disciple should already be a Christian. If you want to reproduce your life in someone, he has to be someone who has God's life in him. This certainly does not mean that you do not spend time with unbelievers. It is to be hoped that some of the people you will build up in and send out for Christ will be those whom you have led to Christ. But in order to be able to take someone through the three phases of discipleship, it is essential that the person be a Christian. One thing you can do if you have many non-Christian contacts is to begin an evangelistic Bible study. From the fruit of the study you can find your "Timothy."

Teachable attitude. It is important that the person you select have a teachable attitude. It is to be hoped that you will have the chance to observe this in the person you are considering. Does the person show a genuine desire to learn? Is there a willingness to submit to being taught? Does the person listen to you when you teach truths? Does he ask questions concerning areas of Christian living? I have not found too many new or young Christians who are unteachable, because they usually want to grow and learn.

Heart for God. Does the person desire to know God better? Does his life show that he is concerned with the things of God? Does he desire to live more for God than for himself? Does he want to allow Christ to change his life? Often, a young Christian will not show externally that he has a desire, or heart, for God. But rather than being anything outward, a heart for God is more an attitude, or spirit, that you need to detect within a person.

Faithfulness. "And the things which you have heard from me in the presence of many witnesses, these entrust to slothful men." Is that what the verse says? No. "These entrust to *faithful men*," 2 Timothy 2:2 says (emphasis added). Foremost in Paul's mind was the fact that God had entrusted him with the gospel message and spiritual truth to be preached everywhere. It was his desire not only to be faithful in distributing those "commodities," but also to see truth passed on to those who would be faithful in receiving it and then preaching and teachng it to others. Paul did not have the kind of time that allowed him to invest his life in slothful, irresponsible people. He wanted to make the best possible use of his time; therefore, he spent it with faithful men.

Listen, discipler. Do not pour your life into someone who is inconsistent in doing assignments or fulfilling little responsibilities, or who shows other signs of unfaithfulness. Be slow to give up on someone, however. There will be times periodically when a person will stumble in this area. The person to look out for is the one whose life is characterized by irresponsibility and unfaithfulness. Do not commit yourself to a discipling relationship with that kind of person. It may be that you will want to spend some time with him in talking through his problem and how he can overcome it. That might be a wise thing to do. But when it comes to selecting your "Timothy," find a person whose life is characterized by faithfulness. It has been my experience that if a person has a teachable attitude and a heart for God, he will not have any problem with being faithful.

Able to keep the time commitment. A person may be teachable, faithful, and have a heart for God; but if he is unable to find the time to meet with you, it will be difficult for the two of you to have a discipling relationship. You should select a person who has the time to meet with you.

WHERE TO FIND DISCIPLES

Where do you find people whom you can challenge to a discipling relationship? Here are some possibilities:

- someone you have led to Christ
- friends
- someone at your job
- neighbors
- someone in your family
- classmates
- someone at your church

CHALLENGING A POTENTIAL DISCIPLE

Now that you have a potential disciple in mind, how do you go about beginning a discipling relationship with him? This is where the challenge comes in. What is a challenge? A challenge is an invitation to be a participant in a specific activity. In this case, the specific activity is a discipling relationship. You are inviting someone to participate in the activity of meeting with you for the purpose of growth.

Why do you need to challenge others? God gives all of His people a desire to grow in Him. Christians, especially young Christians, are so ready for someone to come and lead them. They are waiting to learn, simply needing direction. Unless we who are older in Christ go to them, express our concern for their lives, and give them direction for their growth in Christ, they can become stagnant. They need to be guided and challenged.

But what do you include in a challenge? First, tell the person that you have noticed his desire to grow. Second, tell the person how he can benefit from meeting with you. Third, tell the person your goals. Fourth, tell the person about the time commitment. Fifth, have the person pray about the decision. This last point is essential. You want the potential disciple to determine whether meeting with you is God's will. As he prays about the decision, he will begin to sense the importance of meeting with you.

SAMPLE CHALLENGE

The following is a sample challenge. When you challenge the person you have in mind, you will probably want to say something similar to this. Do not memorize what is suggested here—put it in your own words.

Pat, I want to tell you about something, and I ask that you pray about your possible involvement. In the time I have known you, I have noticed a real desire in your life to know God better and to grow in your relationship with Christ. That attitude certainly pleases God. And Pat, two things that have helped me in my Christian walk have been to understand some essential truths of the Christian faith and to see exactly how God wants to use me in the lives of others. Because of that, I would very much like to meet with Christians such as yourself who show a teachable spirit and a heart for God. My purpose is to help you grow to maturity and then direct you so that you can reproduce your spiritual life in someone else. I would like you to consider meeting with me on a regular basis so that we can both experience growth in our walks with Christ. The time commitment would be _____. Would you pray about this?

SOME POINTERS AS YOU CHALLENGE

Here are a few thoughts that can help you make your challenge effective. First, be enthusiastic as you challenge the person. You do not want to be jumping up and down with joy as you challenge someone, but you certainly do not want to be so serious that all emotion is gone. Have a Spirit-controlled enthusiasm as you challenge the person. That will communicate to the potential disciple the joy and excitement you have in the prospect of meeting with him.

Second, challenge the person at a convenient time. It is not wise to challenge someone while he is waiting for a bus, diving into a pool, or being wheeled into an operating room. Wait until the time is right and the two of you are in a quiet place. Picking the right time and place will communicate to the potential disciple that you consider the possible discipling relationship with him to be important.

Third, make sure the potential disciple understands what you are asking. He needs to know exactly what it is that you are asking him to do.

Fourth, do not minimize the commitment. Decide beforehand the extent of the commitment you will ask of the potential disciple. Whatever you decide upon, do not minimize the commitment when you challenge the person.

Fifth, be prepared in your challenge. How you challenge the individual will affect how he responds. Know exactly what you want to say and how you are going to say it. The challenge will be your first contact with your potential disciple in which you are in the role of a discipler, and it is very important that he understand your intentions in beginning a relationship with him. So be prepared.

7
BUILDING A DISCIPLE

Once the potential disciple has actually become a disciple through the process of selecting and challenging, the building process begins. This chapter focuses on the last three lines of our definition:

Discipling others is the process
by which a Christian with a
life worth emulating
commits himself
for an extended period of time
to a few individuals
who have been
won to Christ, the
purpose being to
aid and guide their
growth to maturity and equip them to
reproduce themselves in a third spiritual generation.

For a disciple to be sufficiently built up in an area of Christian living, three processes must be used: teaching, training, and transforming.[1] Teaching involves knowledge and emphasizes the principles a disciple should know. Training involves skill and emphasizes the practical things a disciple should be able to do. Transforming involves conviction and emphasizes the perspective a disciple should have. The following diagram illustrates the above statements:

---

1. Walter A. Henrichsen, *Disciples Are Made—Not Born* (Wheaton, Ill.: Victor, 1974), pp. 72-74.

These three processes do not necessarily build on each other. They do not have to come in any particular order. As you will see, there is some overlapping, because training includes teaching, and the transforming process takes place in teaching. So the three processes are not exclusive of each other, although for a person to be adequately built up in Christ, all three are necessary. Let's examine separately each of the processes.

TEACHING

Again, teaching involves the communication of knowledge, or principles, and is the foundation of a discipling ministry. A disciple is a learner, one who comes to be taught. Therefore, trying to disciple someone without teaching him is contradictory to the whole purpose of discipling. Matthew 28:20 says that once you have disciples, you are to *teach them*. What are you to teach them? *All* that Jesus commanded. The scope of your teaching should include all that Christ spoke on. This is crucial. The disciple needs the assurance that you will eventually teach him all that he will need to know to grow to maturity.

Look at what a high priority teaching others was to Christ and Paul. Jesus "taught in Capernaum" (John 6:59); in the midst of a feast He went to the Temple and "began to teach" (John 7:14); He went again to the Temple and "began to teach them" (John 8:2); in the region of Judea and beyond the Jordan, "according to His custom, He once more began to teach them" (Mark 10:1); and in the synagogue they were "amazed at His teaching" (Mark 1:22). These and many other Scripture passages point to the importance of teaching in Christ's ministry.

The apostle Paul was no different. He taught the Ephesians "the whole purpose of God" for three years (Acts 20:27-31); in Corinth, "he settled there a year and six months, *teaching* the word of God among them" (Acts 18:11; emphasis added); and in his rented quarters in Rome, he was "teaching concerning the Lord Jesus Christ" (Acts 28:31). That is why Paul could say to the Colossians that his ministry was one of admonishing every man and *teaching* every man (Colossians 1:28).

Both the Lord Jesus Christ and the apostle Paul knew the importance of teaching their followers divine principles. They both knew that all Scripture is profitable (valuable, not worthless) for teaching (it tells us what God requires), reproof (it tells us how we have failed), correction (it tells us what we can do to get right with God and others), and training in righteousness (it enables, or trains, us, with righteousness as its goal (2 Timothy 3:16).

Now that we have seen the importance of teaching, let's examine some principles of teaching.

PRINCIPLES OF REPETITION

One mark of a good teacher is his ability to repeat and remind his disciple of the same truths. Why is that a mark of a good teacher? Because a good teacher realizes how quickly people forget. It is only through repetition that we learn. That is why Paul said to the Philippians, "To write the *same things* again is no trouble to me, and it is a safeguard for you" (Philippians 3:1, emphasis added). Peter also understood this concept, saying, "I shall always be ready to remind you of these things" (2 Peter 1:12). He also wanted to stir up his readers "by way of reminder" (2 Peter 1:13). As you disciple an individual, do not be afraid to repeat the same truths over and over. Do not assume that because the disciple has heard a truth once, he need never hear it again.

PRINCIPLE OF AUTHORITY

One characteristic of Christ's teaching was its authority, which was obvious to His listeners.[2] After the Sermon on the Mount, it was said of Him, "He was teaching them as one having authority" (Matthew 7:29). There was a quality of confidence in the way Jesus spoke to others. He was not apologetic or unsure, but authoritative. That same quality must be communicated to those you disciple. How can you teach authoritatively? You first need to be convinced that the *Bible is the Word of God*, that it is the only

2. Gary Tangeman, "New Testament Principles of Discipleship," Master's thesis, Talbot Theological Seminary, 1975, pp. 35-43.

authoritative book for life, and that it alone contains words of spirit and life. If you are not so convinced, you will not be able to speak with any degree of confidence. Second, if you are to speak authoritatively, you must live what you teach. The most amazing quality of Christ's life was that everything He taught was demonstrated by His life. I know from experience that when I am living a godly life, speaking with authority comes easily; but when sin is in my life, all confidence is gone.

PRINCIPLE OF SIMPLICITY

An effective teacher is able to take a profound truth of Christian living and relate it in simple, easy-to-understand words to his listeners. Christ had this ability. In fact, "The common people heard him gladly" (Mark 12:37, KJV*). Christ had a clear understanding of His listeners' spiritual maturity, and He accommodated His teaching to their level. He never burdened His disciples with information they could not understand. He taught them "as they were able to hear it" (Mark 4:33). As their understanding increased, so, too, did the depth of His teaching. As you disciple, discern the limits of the disciple's understanding and attempt to stay within those limits. There will be times when you will want to introduce new concepts and theological truths that are beyond his understanding in order to stimulate his thinking, but for the most part, keep the teaching simple and at his level of maturity.

PRINCIPLE OF VARIETY

There are basically two approaches you can use when teaching a disciple. The first is the formal approach. This is where you sit down with him and teach him biblical principles. It is a planned, structured time of teaching, before which you have thought through exactly what you want to communicate. When you meet, you might be going through a book, a workbook, or some other planned course of study. This formal approach is definitely a part of a discipling ministry. The Sermon on the Mount seems to be an example of this approach.

The second approach is the informal approach. In this method, the teacher uses the everyday circumstances of life to

* King James Version.

impart spiritual principles. Christ was the master of this approach. In fact, this was His primary method of teaching. Because the disciples were always with Him wherever He went, He was able to use the situations He encounterd as platforms from which to instruct His disciples. To Christ, every circumstance was an opportunity to teach the disciples a principle of living; so wherever He was and whatever the circumstances, He taught. For example, in Luke 21:1-4 Jesus and His disciples were in the Temple area, observing people who were giving their offerings. They observed the rich people, who were, no doubt, giving huge amounts, But when a poor widow came and gave two small, copper coins, what did Jesus say? "That woman sure ministered to my life! Well, men, let's go." No, that is not what He said. In His mind, He probably said, *I want to make sure My men don't miss that one.* He looked at the disciples and told them what had just taken place. The widow had given more than all the others because the rich gave out of their abundance, whereas she gave all she had. Giving is to be sacrificial. Christ seized the opportunity to teach His disciples a truth about giving. He never missed such an opportunity to teach His disciples truths on the nature of godliness. He was able to take any circumstance or conversation and masterfully turn it into an opportunity to teach some spiritual principle. For other examples of this approach in Christ's teaching, look up the following verses: Mark 8:14-21; 9:33-37; Luke 8:22-25; 12:13-34; 13:1-5.

As a discipler, look upon every situation that you encounter with your disciple as an opportunity to teach a spiritual principle. When you are with him, observe his reactions to the things you experience. His response by what he says and does may give you the opportunity to teach a spiritual truth. Also, use the setting you are in to illustrate some thought. Many years ago I was on a college campus with another Christian, and as we were looking at all the students going to their classes, my friend said to me, "Allen, look at all those sheep without a shepherd." I will never forget that moment. That one statement in that particular setting communicated more to me than an hour's message on an appropriate Scripture verse ever could have. Begin now to make the informal approach to teaching a more effective part of your discipling ministry.

PRINCIPLE OF SELF-DISCOVERY

One of the basic principles of learning is that a person retains a truth better when he personally discovers it than he does when he has it taught to him. In teaching or counseling a disciple, whenever possible allow him to discover for himself the principle he should learn and the way to apply it. One way to accomplish this is to ask questions. Let's suppose the disciple comes to you with the problem of worry. How will you teach him? You could take out your notes on worry and tell him the six reasons for not worrying. Or you could take him to Matthew 6:25-34 and ask *him* to read it and have *him* write down the reasons Jesus gives for a Christian to not worry. When he discovers the principles himself he will retain them longer, and he will begin to see that God can speak to *him* through *His Word* (and not just through your notes).

PRINCIPLE OF USE OF SCRIPTURE

When you are teaching a disciple, make it your goal to never teach a biblical principle apart from a verse or passage of Scripture. This will help the disciple see that you desire the Word of God to be the authority and not your own wisdom. His respect for the Scripture will grow as he observes your use of it. Also, he may forget the specific principle you teach, but if he remembers the verse, he will always be able to extract the principle for himself.

Once you have taught the disciple principles from the Word, have you sufficiently built him up in that particular area? No. You must go one step further and train him.

TRAINING

Training is the process by which you help a disciple learn a particular skill. Training emphasizes the practical; it involves showing your disciple how to put into practice the principles you have taught him. Training helps the disciple with the methods of a particular action. For example, you might show him how to study, how to pray, or how to witness. Often we read Matthew 28:20 as if it said, "Teaching them all that I commanded you.' We leave out two very important words when we misread the verse that way. We are to teach them *to observe* all that Chris' commanded. Once the disciple *knows* the commands through your teaching, he needs to know *how to observe* them, that is, apply them in his life. Unfortunately, this aspect of building up a person has been neglected in many Christian circles. For example, most Christians know they should evangelize. They simply need to know *how* to evangelize. Many a Christian knows that he should pour his life into someone else in a discipling relationship. What such a Christian lacks is the practical methodology of discipling. Therefore, training is essential if one is to be built up in Christ. There are four steps in the training process (as described in Chuck Miller's "Discipling Ministry Seminar"[3]).

STEP 1: THE DISCIPLER DOES IT

Throughout this book we have been talking about step 1. Nothing will happen in the disciple's life unless it is first happening in yours. If the disciple is to learn the skills of the Christian life and ministry, you must be effective in them first. Looking at the ministries of the Lord Jesus Christ and Barnabas, we see this step in operation. In Mark 2:1-12, Jesus was in Capernaum, and we see Him engaged in the ministry of healing. Some of the disciples were with Him at that point, but He had not officially called the twelve, so *He was carrying on the ministry*. In Acts 11:22-24, we note the ministry of Barnabas, who was encouraging the Antiochian Christians to remain true to the Lord. Barnabas was alone at that time, *doing* the work of the ministry. So we see that the task of training must begin with you, the discipler. You must be doing the work of the ministry. You must learn how to evangelize. You must learn how to teach. You must learn how to counsel. You must take every opportunity available to learn the skills of the ministry. The first step in training the disciple is that you must become proficient in the skill you want to teach him.

STEP 2: THE DISCIPLER DOES IT, AND THE DISCIPLE
IS WITH HIM

Once a particular skill has been developed in your life, you are able to use it in the presence of the disciple. We see this step in Christ's life in Mark 4, which describes His teaching of the multitudes. Who was with Him? His disciples. They were with

3. Chuck Miller, *Discipling Ministry Seminar* (seminar notebook), 1976, p. 65. Barnabas, Inc., P.O. Box 16122, Irvine, CA 92714.

Him, watching Him. Also in Mark 5, the disciples were with Christ as He dealt with the Gerasene demoniac, healed the woman with the hemorrhage, and raised Jairus's daughter. In Acts 11:25—13:8, Barnabas was no longer working in the ministry alone, but he had a companion, Paul. And in these chapters, Barnabas was definitely the leader. Barnabas led the work, and Paul was with him.

Several principles are in operation here. The first one is the *principle of observation*. When you do the work of the ministry in the presence of your disciple, he has the chance to observe you and thus acquire information about how to perform the task. If you want him to learn the skill of witnessing to others, you take him with you when you witness so that he can observe you. If you want him to learn how to lead a small group, you get him involved in a group you are leading so that he can watch you do it. At this point you are still leading, but the disciple is in such a position that he is able to observe you.

The principle of observation points to another principle in step 2, the *principle of example*. If the disciple is to be with you, watching you, then you must be someone whom he desires to follow; that is, you must be a pattern, or example, that is worthy of emulation.

After you learn to do something yourself and then do it with the disciple watching you, you are ready for the third step in the training process.

STEP 3: THE DISCIPLE DOES IT, AND THE DISCIPLER IS WITH HIM

In this step, the roles of step 2 are reversed, and you are watching the disciple. He is now doing the work, and you are observing him, giving him on-site supervision. In Mark 6:30-44, Jesus has His disciples doing the work of the ministry. They were given the task of distributing food to the people. They were in a position of meeting the needs of the multitude, something they had previously observed in Jesus' life. In Acts 13:9-50 we note a definite change in the roles of Barnabas and Paul. When Luke wrote this passage, his reference to the two men became "Paul and Barnabas" (see vv. 13, 42, 43, 46, 50). Paul had become the leader, and Barnabas was with Paul.

In step 3, several principles become apparent. One principle is the *principle of challenge,* or *delegation.* When the disciple has observed you sufficiently, there comes a point at which he needs to be "kicked out of the nest" and given responsibilities. Therefore, you challenge the disciple to take on a responsibility. Once the disciple has watched you lead a small-group discussion, you say, "Next week I want you to lead the group." Or after the disciple has observed your witnessing to others, you say, "Now it's your turn to approach a person and give him the gospel."

Another principle is the *principle of equipping*, or *training*. Part of step 3 is your equipping the disciple to develop and use particular skills. By the time you reach step 3, the disciple has been taught the principles regarding the particular areas being discussed (teaching) and has observed you in the process of using the skills (step 2 of training). He simply needs to be trained in the methodologies. As you equip the disciple, you will begin to see the importance of step 2, because when you equip him, telling him what he needs to know to exercise the particular skills, you will often say, "Now remember how I did it." Your equipping of him will take you back to his observations of you.

A third principle seen in step 3 is the *principle of involvement*. Nothing takes the place of having the disciple actually doing the work. This is how he learns—by doing it—not by perpetually watching someone else. He will not learn simply by hearing the words of the discipler or watching the life of the discipler. He will learn best by getting *involved*. If you ever want to get personally excited in a discipling ministry, get your disciple into step 3. This is when unbelievable joy is found—when the disciple puts into practice what you have taught him. Watching one of the men I am discipling witness to someone, give his testimony to a group, or lead a small-group discussion is very satisfying.

A fourth principle in step 3 is the *principle of evaluation*. After you have been with the disciple, watching him exercise a particular skill, you are able to evaluate him. This is one of those teaching moments. Correct the disciple's weaknesses. No doubt he will fail many times in performing a task or using a skill, but give him a chance to fail. In Mark 9:18, the disciples failed by not being able to cast out a demon. Jesus told them why they failed, but then He gave them insight into how they could avoid failure in the future. This time of evaluation also gives you the opportunity to encourage your disciple by pointing out his strengths.

Before we move to step 4, let's review:

Step 1: The discipler does it.
Step 2: The discipler does it, and the disciple is with him.
Step 3: The disciple does it, and the discipler is with him.

STEP 4: THE DISCIPLE DOES IT, AND THE DISCIPLER IS
IN THE BACKGROUND

Once you do something, such as witness, and the disciple has watched you and you have watched him, he is then able to do that work with you in the background. In Mark 9, Jesus and three of the disciples were on the mount of transfiguration, but the other nine men were down below, involved in step 4—they were "doing," but Christ was not there. In Matthew 10:5-42, Jesus sent the disciples out to minister by themselves while He went His own way (Matthew 11:1) to teach and preach in other cities. Also, in Acts 15:36-41 the time had come for Paul and Barnabas to go their separate ways. The circumstances of their separation were unfortunate, but nevertheless Paul was at a point beyond which he was able to minister without Barnabas's presence.

One principle is significant in step 4, and that is the *principle of reproduction*. When a person has reached step 4, reproduction has taken place in the particular skill for which he is being trained. Reproduction is the disciples of Jesus in the book of Acts after Jesus had ascended. Reproduction is Paul ministering throughout the world without Barnabas. Reproduction is a man I discipled several years ago, now many miles away, ministering to others. That is the goal of the training process—to bring a person to the point at which he is able to do a particular job or exercise a particular skill in ministering to others without the discipler being present.

After you have taught the disciple the principles in a particular area (teaching), and after you have trained the disciple to do the work (training), has the building process been completed? What assurance do you have that the disciple will *continue* in the activity once you are no longer around? A third process in building up someone is needed.

TRANSFORMING

Transforming the disciple is the process by which you help him to gain a conviction, or perspective, on some aspect of Christian growth. You are seeking to change the disciple's sense of values and plant convictions in him that will affect his whole life. You desire that he gain God's perspective on a particular area, such as evangelism, discipling others, or prayer. This final process in building up a disciple is crucial, because no matter how much knowledge (teaching) and skill (training) he has, he will not continue in an activity unless he is transformed on the inside, that is, unless he gains a conviction that the particular activity is essential. When I leave the one I am discipling, I want him to *continue* doing what I instructed and trained him to do, and that will not happen unless the internal transformation takes place.

How do you transform a disciple's life? How do you help the Christian develop his own convictions?

FILL THE DISCIPLE WITH INFORMATION ON THE SUBJECT

To help the disciple gain his own convictions on some part of the Christian life, begin by guiding him to Bible passages that will help him see how God looks at the particular issue.[4] Doing an in-depth study of Paul's heart for the lost deepened my convictions on the need to evangelize. The value of having the disciple do the study is that he will come to his *own* conclusions, with the result that the convictions he gains will be his. In addition to redirecting him to Bible passages, you might have him read books on the particular subject. If you want him to be transformed in the area of prayer, for example, have him read books on prayer, such as *Power Through Prayer*, by E. M. Bounds, or books about men of prayer, such as George Müller.

ESTABLISH AN ATMOSPHERE CONDUCIVE TO INFLUENCING THE DISCIPLE

When I was on staff with a Christian organization, simply being on a college campus developed within me an inner conviction that evangelism is important because I was seeing the need

4. Henrichsen, p. 74.

firsthand. I was put in a situation in which God had the raw materials to instill within me the desire to give witness of my faith. Being in the environment of a seminary gave me the conviction to be a diligent student of God's Word. The whole concept here is that of "caught not taught"; that is, you need to establish an atmosphere in which the disciple will naturally develop godly perspectives.

ASK GOD TO CONFIRM THE TRUTH IN THE DISCIPLE'S LIFE

As mentioned in a previous chapter, we tend to pray as the last resort. But prayer needs to be the continual activity of a discipler. Do you desire your disciple to be self-motivated in evangelism, ministering to the needs of Christians, or involved in any other activity? Pray for him. Ask God to give the disciple a conviction about the importance of those and other areas.

BE A CONSISTENT EXAMPLE TO THE DISCIPLE

We have already discussed establishing an atmosphere in which something can be caught. The consistent example of your life may well be the best motivation you can give a disciple to gain right convictions in Christian living. Again, nothing is a substitute for the example of a godly life. When you are gone, the disciple will never forget the qualities he saw lived out in your life.

CHALLENGE THE DISCIPLE TO BE OBEDIENT IN THE PARTICULAR AREA

Training the disciple to be obedient to God's commands is one of the most effective ways of building conviction in his life. When I was obedient to God by praying to Him, He developed a conviction in my life about the necessity of prayer through the results I saw. The significance and importance of studying the Bible became apparent to me as I was obedient to God and began studying His Word. Obedience, with the resultant blessing of God in my life, developed within me the motivation to study.

8

INTERACTING WITH A DISCIPLE

Once a discipling relationship has begun, how does the discipler go about interacting with the disciple so that maximum growth can take place in the disciple's life? In this chapter, we want to look at five principles of interacting with the disciple. The parts of our definition of discipling that this chapter will cover are the italicized phrases:

> Discipling others is the process
> by which a Christian with a
> life worth emulating
> *commits himself*
> *for an extended period of time*
> to a few individuals
> who have been
> won to Christ, the
> purpose being to
> *aid and guide their*
> growth to maturity and equip them to
> reproduce themselves in a third spiritual generation.

PRINCIPLE 1. THE DISCIPLER IS TO LOVE THE DISCIPLE

It is very difficult to disciple people effectively unless you have convinced them that you love them. When you have convinced them of your love, the process of making mature people out of them becomes easier. Why did the disciples follow Jesus? Because they never doubted that He loved them. He demonstrated His love for them in practical ways. John MacArthur has made a significant statement concerning love for the disciple: "When I fail to really commit myself in love to somebody, I never see the real fruit of discipleship in their life.

Never!"[1] What a powerful statement. But how can you show love to the disciple? It should be demonstrated in two ways, which are discussed in the following paragraphs.

BY PERSONAL SACRIFICE

Howard Hendricks has said, "If you want your disciple to bleed, then you must hemorrhage." Discipling others is work, and it demands a sense of personal sacrifice. Results in the disciple's life require sacrifice in yours. Look at Paul's life and words: "And I will most gladly spend and be expended for your souls" (2 Corinthians 12:15). Paul said that he was willing to be expended, willing to be exhausted—worn out in his labors, his life consumed in serving them—if it meant their welfare. He was saying, "I am willing to spend my strength, time, life, and all that I have for your welfare. I am willing to submit to any expense." That is what loving disciples means.

You, as a discipler, need to make Paul's kind of commitment. If you truly love your disciples, you will spend time and money and anything else to see them mature. If you are too busy or too preoccupied with your own needs and interests, not willing to give your total energy to those disciples, you will never see them grow to be all that they can be. If you give of yourself to disciples, then they in return will give of themselves to what you believe in. Discipling demands sacrifice, and that means hard work.

BY PERSONAL CONCERN

Personal concern is the other way your love for disciples is demonstrated. The concern of the shepherd must be for the sheep and not himself. Each disciple should be able to say about you, "Thank You, Lord, that there is at least one person who is concerned about my growth to maturity."

Paul's life clearly illustrates this personal concern. For example, we notice in Acts 14 that Paul and his companions were persecuted in Lystra, Iconium, and Antioch for preaching the

1. John MacArthur, sermon delivered at Fall Mobilization Conference, Campus Crusade for Christ, October 1975, San Bernardino, Calif. For a list of tape recordings by John MacArthur on the subject of discipling, write to Word of Grace Communications, Box 4000, Panorama City, CA 91412.

gospel, and yet we find them returning to those cities. Why? Because they loved to suffer? No. Their desire was to strengthen the souls of the disciples (vv. 21-22). Their love was made manifest by their personal concern. In Acts 15:36, Paul desires to revisit the other cities to "see how they [the brethren] are." That showed his concern. He passed through the Galatian region and Phrygia, strengthening the disciples (Acts 18:23). For a period of three years he taught and admonished the Ephesian saints (Acts 20:31). It was his desire to present the Corinthian believers "as a pure virgin" to Christ (2 Corinthians 11:2). He was in labor until Christ was formed in the Galatians (Galatians 4:19). Even though being with Christ would have been better, he continued ministering to the Philippians, whose maturity he desired (Philippians 1:21-26). He exhorted, encouraged, and implored the Thessalonians that they might walk in a manner worthy of God (1 Thessalonians 2:11-12).

Paul's concern was for the spiritual welfare of the believers. Paul's concern revealed the depth and commitment of his love. Are your sacrifice and concern similar to Paul's?

What can you do in a practical way so that the disciples can see personal sacrifice and concern in you? Here are a few suggestions:

Be available to the disciple. Being available means a sacrifice of time. Your availability will show the disciple that you consider him to be important. It will show him that you consider his needs to be significant enough that you would sacrifice meeting your own needs at the moment in order to meet his. I will never forget the example a married couple was to me in this area. I would go over to their house and ask them questions, and I would usually stay late. And even though they had to wake up early the next morning, they continued to meet my needs. Their constant availability to me at any hour demonstrated their love for me.

Pray for the disciple. Praying for him is one of the most loving things you can do for a disciple. If you truly love him, you will be constantly taking his needs before the Father. In fact, you will find that praying for the disciple will actually increase your concern for him. You will find that you become more committed and involved in that for which you pray. So, let's all be like Epaphras, who was always laboring for the Colossians in his prayers to the end that they would stand perfect and fully assured in the will of God.

Telephone the disciple. A phone call once in a while is a very practical way of demonstrating your love for the disciple. Call the disciple and see how he is doing. This will show the disciple that you consider his needs to be important enough to merit the time for a call.

Spend time with the disciple. Your time involvement with the disciple will be discussed under principle 3.

Listen to the disciple who is in need. Have you ever wondered why God gave us two ears and just one mouth? Could it possibly be that He wants us to do twice as much listening as speaking? There are far too many "speakers" in Christendom today and very few "listeners." When the disciple has something on his mind that needs to be discussed, show your love for him by listening to what he has to say.

Affirm the disciple. Affirmation is telling someone that he is important to you and to God. Affirmation takes place when we see each other as valuable and worthwhile and then communicate this to each other. How desperately we need this in the Body of Christ. There are many Christians who have never been affirmed by parents, friends, or other Christians. Consequently, they grow up thinking that they are insignificant or even worthless. The next time you see the disciple, communicate to him the value and worth that you see in him.

Confront the disciple with his sin. Sin does nothing but destroy an individual. Therefore, if you love the disciple, it will be necessary for you to confront him with his sin. More on this point later.

Be faithful in your preparation for the time with the disciple. Inadequate preparation usually reveals an attitude of lack of concern for the disciple's needs. Be diligent. Do the best you can. That will communicate to the disciple the depth of your concern.

Give the disciple gifts. At times you might want to buy your disciple Christian books or tape recordings, or else pay his way to a camp or conference.

Ask God for wisdom in meeting the disciple's needs. Your desire for God's wisdom in dealing with him is not something that the disciple can always *see* in you. There might be times in your prayers with the disciple when you might say, "Lord, I so want to meet Joe's needs. I ask You to give me the wisdom to know how to more effectively encourage him, motivate him, and teach him." When the disciple hears you praying that prayer, he cannot help but be convinced that you have his best interests in mind.

PRINCIPLE 2. THE DISCIPLER MUST MINISTER TO THE TOTAL PERSON

Luke 2:52, a much quoted verse in regard to the subject of ministering to the whole person, points out four areas of growth in Christ's life. It states that He grew in wisdom (mental), stature (physical), favor with God (spiritual), and favor with man (social). As you disciple an individual, you need to think of developing each of those areas in his life. Your ministry to the disciple needs to be a *total* ministry. To meet his spiritual needs to the exclusion of his social or mental needs shows a lack of understanding of the wholeness of man. Your view of the disciple must be a "whole" view. You must see him as one who has needs, not only in the spiritual area but also in the physical, social, and mental areas. Because the rest of this book emphasizes the spiritual area, let's here discuss the physical, social, and mental aspects.

THE PHYSICAL AREA

The physical part of life is often overlooked by disciplers, yet it is crucial. One's spiritual outlook and behavior are much affected by one's physical conditioning. One item to be considered under this point is exercise. If the disciple is sluggish and unmotivated in spiritual things, his lack of physical exercise may be the problem. You may have to point that out to him. Another area of concern is weight. Perhaps the disciple needs to lose or gain weight. His eating habits may have to be examined. Personal hygiene is another area to be considered. Unfortunately, it is not always pleasant to confront others who have problems with personal hygiene. Yet it has to be done, and the discipler is usually the best person to bring up the topic. Other areas to consider are the disciple's sleeping habits and the clothes he wears.

THE SOCIAL AREA

Someone has said that the Christian life can be narrowed down to one term—relationships. You will find very quickly that much of your counsel to your disciple will deal with this area. You might have to help the disciple learn to get along more effectively with his parents, brother, sister, employer, employee, spouse, or child. If the disciple is in the dating years, you will have to help him think through relationships with members of the opposite sex.

If it is necessary to spend weeks or even months talking through a problem with relationships in the disciple's life, do so. Do not think that you have not accomplished anything in the disciple's life if the two of you have not memorized Scripture or gone through some lesson plan. Deal with the current need in his life. You may have to confront him with problems in his life that could hamper his relationships with others. For example, he may be very shy, too talkative, or overbearing. He may have to be taught social etiquette. Ask God to give you a sensitivity to the needs of the disciple in this area.

I remember one man who had difficulty carrying on a conversation with others, especially those whom he had just met. At a home Bible study, he would rarely talk to strangers. So when I met with him for a one-on-one session, we worked on his problem. I pretended that I was a first-time visitor at a home Bible study, and he was to start a conversation with me. He started asking me questions, but after about thirty seconds, he said, "I don't know what else to say." We went back over our thirty-second-long conversation and analyzed it, and I told him that his problem was that each question he had asked related to a completely different topic. He did not dwell on the subject and "milk" it for what he could. So we tried again, and believe it or not, the conversation lasted quite a long time. And now he has no problems talking with anyone. That short training session gave him the confidence he needed to approach people.

THE MENTAL AREA

Few disciplers think of developing the mental area of a disciple's life, but it is an important area. One concern under this point is the reading habits of the disciple. I have found that disciples who are readers show faster growth in their Christian walk than nonreaders. Why? Readers, by constantly reading Christian books, put principles and spiritual truths into their minds that the Holy Spirit can use to conform them to Christ. Challenge the disciple to read good Christian books, or any book that will encourage him to think.

Address yourself to the total disciple, not just one aspect of his life. Become familiar with his needs. Realize that the needs will vary according to the disciple's age, sex, marital status, employment status, and living arrangement (i.e., whether he lives with parents, a spouse, a roommate, or by himself).

PRINCIPLE 3. THE DISCIPLER MUST SPEND TIME WITH THE DISCIPLE

One word that I have used repeatedly concerning the discipling ministry is *time*. There is no escaping it: the discipler, if he is to see anything take place in the disciple's life, must spend time with the disciple. That was obviously Christ's method, as His calling of the twelve was a call to a personal association with Himself. Jesus "appointed twelve, that they might be *with Him*" (Mark 3:14, emphasis added). And how were His disciples known? They were not known by their rituals or their knowledge, but instead they were known by being *with Christ* (Acts 4:13). Repeatedly, we see Christ and His disciples together. In the land of Judea, He was spending time *with them* (John 3:22). On a mountain by the Sea of Galilee, He sat *with His disciples* (John 6:3). He withdrew to the sea *with His disciples* (Mark 3:7). He went to the villages of Caesarea Philippi *with His disciples* (Mark 8:27).

How much time should a discipler spend with a disciple? The answer is very easy—as much as possible. But if it is impossible to spend a great amount of time with the disciple, do not panic. Your schedule may allow you to spend only one hour per week with him. If that is the case, then make that time count. Supplement that hour with phone calls and personal notes.

Here are some practical things that you and the disciple can do together:

- eat out together
- exercise together
- shop together
- go to church together
- travel together

- pray together
- witness together
- go to sporting events together
- if both of you are single, live together
- cook together
- do homework together

Whatever I am doing, especially if I am ministering to others, I have a principle that I like to follow. It can be stated in three words: *never go alone*. Wherever I go, I like to take one of my men with me. Some time ago, a church youth group asked me to come and speak to their high school and college students. Immediately I asked two of the men I was discipling to go with me. Another church asked me to come and sing for an evening service. Again, two of the men went with me. I sang for the junior high and high school department at my church and asked one of the men I was discipling to go with me. So if you are involved in various ministries, take the disciple with you.

What is the value of spending time with the disciple? First, he will be able to see you in different situations. He will see how the Christian life is worked out in your life. He will see how you react to different situations. It is possible that a disciple can see only the serious side of the discipler, especially if the only contact is in a discipling group. But by spending much time with you in different situations, the disciple will be able to get a more balanced view of you. He will be able to see different facets of your personality.

A second value is that unity will develop. The principle here is that of supporting one another. When those men went with me to those speaking and singing engagements, I felt as if we were a team. It encouraged me tremendously to have them with me. I knew that they were truly interested in what I was doing, and their support brought us closer together as brothers. But brotherhood is not only the disciple's supporting you; you support him. If the disciple is involved in certain activities, go to them. Let the disciple know that you are interested in him. When one of the men I discipled graduated from high school, I went to the ceremony. I must be honest with you and say that I am not too thrilled about school graduations, especially about hearing nine hundred names read. But it was important for me to be there. It was a high point in the disciple's life, and any sacrifice I could have made to be with him would have been worth it. When you spend time with the disciple by supporting him, a sense of closeness and unity develops.

A third value of time spent with the disciple is that learning takes place through association. When the disciple spends time with you, he cannot help but learn your ways and follow your walk. Why did Jesus call men to Himself? He called them so that they could be with Him and also learn to preach the gospel. It is obvious that by spending time with Jesus, they could not help but become fishers of men.

Think of Elijah and Elisha. For eight years they were together, traveling, eating, and ministering side by side. When Elijah left the scene, was Elisha prepared? Absolutely. In similar fashion, Joshua was so close to Moses that it was said of him that he did not leave Moses' tent. Moses' characteristics would naturally be reproduced in Joshua.

A story is told about the Italians who, in 1935, occupied Ethiopia and expelled all the Protestant missionaries.[2] For seven years no one knew what was going on in Ethiopia. When the missionaries were expelled, they left behind 60 believers in 3 congregations. One of those believers had been a suitcase carrier for one of the missionary evangelists, following the missionary wherever he went. In 1942 the missionaries went back to Ethiopia and found, not 60 believers in 3 congregations, but 18,000 believers in 155 congregations. Do you know what had happened? The suitcase boy had said to himself. "The missionaries are gone. I will do what they did." So he got himself a suitcase boy and traveled from city to city, proclaiming the gospel, just as he had seen the missionaries do. Learning does indeed take place through association.

A fourth value of spending time with the disciple is that during informal times, the disciple often becomes more open and honest about his victories and problems. What is not discussed in a structured, formal setting in a house may be more

2. Jim White, "Endurance in the Great Commission," cassette. The Navigators, P.O. Box 20, Colorado Springs, CO 80901.

easily discussed in a casual, informal conversation at a park or on a drive.

Another value of spending a large amount of time with the disciple in different activities is that the disciple will begin to see that you consider him to be more than just a person who is part of your weekly calendar. Spending time with him communicates to him that you want to be his friend.

PRINCIPLE 4. THE DISCIPLER MUST GIVE A REALISTIC VIEW OF HIMSELF TO THE DISCIPLE

One danger in a discipling ministry is that you, as a discipler, can easily communicate to those whom God has entrusted to your care an image of perfection—you can appear to be a spiritual giant who has all the answers. That is not giving your disciples a realistic view of yourself. The disciples need to know of your joys *and* sorrows, of your victories *and* defeats. They need to know of your humanness. None of us is perfect; we all face the same temptations and frustrations. We all have a common enemy, Satan. We are all in the Christian life together. We are all pilgrims. The discipler is made of everyday clay, just like the disciple. You must be honest with the disciples and not put up a front. Let's look at why projecting a realistic image of yourself is so important.

YOU CAN EXPERIENCE TRUE FELLOWSHIP

Many a discipler has missed out on rich fellowship with his disciples simply because the sharing of the burdens went only one way, from the disciple to the discipler. Since when is the ministry of the Body of Christ one-sided? We are to minister to one another. As a discipler, you *need* the disciples, and you must not think that your being a guardian means that you must always give and never receive. If you view disciples as people who cannot minister to you, take heed. Your relationships with them can easily become businesslike and never develop into friendships.

Two verses from 2 Corinthians 7 absolutely amaze me. We tend to think of Paul as a strong, independent, and aggressive man who always seemed to be needed by others but who never needed anyone himself. But look at verse 5: "For even when we came into Macedonia our flesh had no rest, but we were afflicted on every side: conflicts without, fears within." Paul was saying that he was hurting deep inside. He was revealing his humanness. Now look at verse 6: "But God who comforts the depressed, comforted us by the coming of Titus." Who comforted Paul? Titus. Who was Titus? Paul's disciple. The disciple ministered to the discipler.

You need the prayer support and comfort of the individuals you are discipling. The men I disciple know of my weaknesses and pray for me. I trust that you will not forfeit a rich and meaningful experience of fellowship by not being open with those you disciple.

FREEDOM IN LIVING THE CHRISTIAN LIFE CAN EXIST

How can there be freedom in living the Christian life? Let's look first at the discipler's life. When the discipler reveals his weaknesses to the disciple, the attitude of having to perform for the disciple disappears. It took me several years of ministering to people before I realized that I had the freedom to fail before others. How could I possibly reveal weaknesses to the men I was discipling and expect them to follow me? was the way I had thought. Because of that attitude, I kept my faults to myself and hid them from others so that I would appear to be perfect and "spiritual."

Let me tell you, it is impossible to appear perfect before others. It takes effort and a lot of acting to do that. But what freedom there is in living the Christian life when you can be honest with the disciple and tell him that you, too, have feet of clay. Honesty makes unnecessary the "performance" kind of living, in which you are trying to be something before the disciple that you never can be, and replaces it with a sense of open and honest living, in which the disciple knows that you are not perfect and that you, too, can sin. The issue is how you want the disciple to perceive you. Do you want him to think of you as the Bionic Discipler who never fails (I certainly hope not) or as a fellow pilgrim who is beset with the same temptations, struggles, and weaknesses as he is?

Revealing your weaknesses will develop within the disciple a sense of freedom in living the Christian life. Why is that the case? Guess what will happen when you begin to disclose the struggles and pressures in your life? The disciple will say, "I didn't know anyone was like me. I thought I was the only one who had problems. I guess I am not that abnormal." Your openness will free him to live the Christian life with the knowledge that he is not the only one who struggles.

TRUST IS DEVELOPED

When you reveal your weaknesses to the disciple, it tells the disciple that you consider your relationship with him to be deep enough that you can entrust him with information about yourself. It lets the disciple know that you trust him.

HONESTY IS THE RESULT

Revealing weaknesses and struggles lets the disciple know that you desire the relationship to be one of honesty, openness, and frankness. A relationship will not grow unless the two individuals in it are honest with each other.

We have looked at why it is important for a discipler to give the disciple a realistic view of himself. But remember that balance is necessary. You do not want to be an individual who reveals nothing but struggles to the exclusion of the joys you experience. And you certainly do not want to discuss only your victories. It is to be hoped that as a discipler you have reached the point in your life at which trials and circumstances do not utterly defeat you and leave you wallowing in the depths of despair. The disciple does not need *that* kind of example to follow. He does need to see you trusting God while you are in the trial. He needs to see you walking by faith as you experience pressures. He needs to see you applying biblical solutions to your struggles and weaknesses. If the pattern of your life is one of constant frustration and depression every time a pressure hits you, you should not now be involved in a discipling ministry. Wait until your walk with the Lord is somewhat more stable and consistent.

PRINCIPLE 5. THE DISCIPLER IS TO COUNSEL THE DISCIPLE

Much of the disciple's growth will come from your counsel to him according to his need at a particular time. Why? When he has a particular need, the disciple is ready to listen to you, learn the principle, and then apply it.

Because counseling is aimed at the immediate needs of the disciple, an atmosphere of honesty and openness must be established. Unless you establish such an atmosphere in your relationship with the disciple, very little growth will take place because he will not want to reveal his immediate needs and struggles.

If I am sick, unless I am willing to go to the doctor, reveal my sickness to him, allow him to ask me questions concerning my sickness, and allow him to examine me, I will not be healed. The same is true of the disciple. For him to be healed, he must be willing to open up. How can that open and honest atmosphere be developed? Here are six ways:

By showing personal concern. I asked one fellow I was discipling, "Why can you be so honest with me?"

"Allen," he said, "it's obvious that you love me and are concerned for me. You sacrifice for me."

When you have convinced the disciple that you have his best interests in mind, openness and honesty will follow naturally.

By revealing your weaknesses. We just looked at the importance of being open with the disciple. Disclosing your weaknesses tells him that you trust him with that information. That will then encourage his openness with you.

By making the disciple sense that you are a friend and not a part-time tutor. Openness is a result of relationships that have depth to them. And certainly, depth is impossible if the relationship stays at a teacher-pupil level, where your commitment to each other is just one hour per week. When the disciple senses that your perception of him is more than just an "appointment," that it is a commitment to be a friend, openness is not far away. The image of a part-time tutor connotes coldness, structure, formality, and the teaching of facts. Friendship connotes warmth, the sharing of lives, and openness.

By being credible. If you are living a consistent, believable life before your disciple, you will be respected. If you are respected, you will be trusted. If you are trusted, the disciple will not fear opening up to you.

By being a listener. What often keeps a disciple from opening up and revealing his life is that he is not being heard. Develop the art of listening, and you will be amazed at the way the relationship with the disciple will grow.

By accepting the disciple. For openness and honesty to be developed, an atmosphere of acceptance needs to be established. Why is that so? To find out, let's think through our relationship with God. Why can we be honest with God? Because we know He accepts us. Divulging our weaknesses, struggles, and sins to God can never threaten the love relationship that exists between ourselves and Him. We have that sense of security with God because we know that even though He disapproves of the sin, He accepts us in Christ. The disciple needs to have that same sense of acceptance and security with you, regardless of what his life has been like or is like now. Walt Henrichsen expresses this idea of acceptance very well:

> I remember when I was growing up that one of the things I appreciated from my father was the fact that I could always talk with him about any subject that was on my mind without fear of being misunderstood or reprimanded. . . . Often there are things on our hearts that we would like to talk to someone about, but we are apprehensive simply because we are afraid of being misunderstood. When following up a Christian, it is essential that he feels free to share his doubts, fears, and personal problems no matter how intimate they may be, without feeling he will be condemned or rejected because of them.[3]

What does accepting the disciple mean in a practical way? Consider three points. First, accepting the disciple means not showing external surprise when the young Christian tells you about something wrong that he has done. If he divulges his sin, do not scream back at him, *"You did what?"* That obviously does not communicate acceptance.

Second, acceptance means being available in times of discomfort or distress. This communicates your acceptance of him because it shows your concern for him when matters are not so comfortable in his life.

3. Walter A. Henrichsen, *Disciples Are Made—Not Born* (Wheaton, Ill.: Victor, 1974), p. 89.

Third, acceptance means telling the disciple that you love him. Although actions are necessary, the disciple often needs to be reassured verbally. Do not be afraid to tell him that you love him.

Besides developing honesty and openness, the discipler must be ready to confront the disciple who is involved in sin. It is easy for the relationship in a discipling ministry to be so friendship oriented that the spiritual leader and guardian role disappears. When that happens, the tendency is for the discipler to become nonauthoritative. But one of the responsibilities of a discipler is to confront the new believer who is involved in sin. The biblical term relating to this is admonishment. To admonish is to criticize lovingly a wrongdoing, the intent being to change the disciple's practices.

The concept of admonishment is expressed in Colossians 1:28: "And we proclaim Him, admonishing every man and teaching every man with all wisdom, that we may present every man complete in Christ." Paul saw his ministry in the lives of people as encompassing a twofold emphasis: (1) teaching them divine principles, putting truth into their minds; and (2) admonishing them when wrong, "taking out" behavior that was not pleasing to God. First Corinthians 4:14 also speaks of the admonishment ministry: "I do not write these things to shame you, but to admonish you as my beloved children."

The intent of admonishment is not to destroy the disciple but to see him changed. And remember that it is your responsibility as a discipler to help the disciple grow in Christlikeness. Therefore, when you see sin in his life, it will be necessary for you to confront him with the fact that his action or attitude is wrong. Admonishing someone certainly is not a popular thing to do, but if you love the disciple, it is absolutely necessary that you confront him with his sin. It is difficult, but it will produce definite, beneficial changes in the long run.

Here are some principles to follow in your counseling ministry:

Use the Bible in counseling. One of the most important things your disciple needs is for you to tie his problem to a scriptural solution. Counseling him from your own wisdom will have an effect, but not a long-lasting effect. He may soon forget the truths you teach him, but he will always have the Scripture there to direct and teach him. So every time the disciple has a need, your first course of action, after you have listened to him, is to get your Bible and point him to scriptural solutions. After all, God will honor His words, not yours. It is through the "encouragement of the Scriptures" that we have hope (Romans 15:4). It is Scripture that is "profitable for teaching, for reproof, for correction, for training in righteousness; that the man of God may be adequate, equipped for every good work" (2 Timothy 3:16-17).

Never tell anyone the personal things revealed by the disciple. That should be obvious. What is disclosed in confidence should never be told to anyone.

Make sure your motive of personal concern in listening to the struggles of the disciple does not turn into curiosity. There is always a temptation because of our flesh to have impure motives in listening to disciples' weaknesses. On the outside, we can appear to be most concerned, but we know that at times concern can turn into curiosity very quickly.

Do not let the disciple give a detailed explanation of the sin or problem. Words paint pictures. For example, imagine a sunny day up in the mountains. There is a small lake, with a lush forest surrounding it. Out on the lake is a rowboat, with a man in it doing some fishing.

Those few sentences have painted a picture in your mind. The disciple, if allowed to give a detailed account of his sin, will paint pictures that stay in your mind. Those pictures then become the raw material that the flesh uses to tempt you. Do not permit detailed accounts of sin.

9

THE ONE-ON-ONE MEETING

In chapter 2, "The Definition of Discipling," it was pointed out that one mark of a discipling relationship is direction—there is a purpose in the relationship because you want to get the disciple to the goals of maturity and multiplication. Consequently, the format that helps you attain those goals is a regular, personal, organized time with the disciple, what I call a one-on-one meeting. This chapter, therefore, deals with the ninth line of our definition of discipling.

Discipling others is the process
by which a Christian with a
life worth emulating
commits himself
for an extended period of time
to a few individuals
who have been
won to Christ, the
purpose being to
aid and guide their
growth to maturity and equip them to
reproduce themselves in a third spiritual generation.

The question we will be answering in this chapter is, What do I do when I meet with the disciple? If you were to ask that question of ten people involved in discipling, you would probably get ten different responses, although there would be some common elements in their answers. There certainly is not just one way of approaching this topic, so what I propose is simply one of many directions a discipler can take when meeting with a disciple. For the remainder of this chapter, we will examine four parts of a one-on-one meeting:

- opening prayer
- discussion time
- lesson time
- conversational prayer

START WITH PRAYER

To get your mind and the disciple's mind prepared for the interaction to follow, it is wise for you, the discipler, to start the meeting with prayer, asking God to make the time meaningful.

HAVE A DISCUSSION TIME

After you have prayed, have a discussion time. Tell each other what God has done the past week. Discuss the victories and the defeats. Tell one another about answers to prayer. You might want to talk about how the truths of last week's lesson were applied during the week. You might also want to discuss evangelistic opportunities you have had, that is, opportunities you had to talk to people about Christ. Remember, the conversation is not one-sided. You are both relating experiences, which makes this part of the meeting a very rich time.

You also want to remember to be flexible during this conversational time. It may be that as you start discussing your lives, the disciple may mention something that happened in the previous week that needs immediate attention. If you have to spend the rest of the time ministering to him, do so. The one-on-one meeting is to be your servant. Do not let it control you. You control it.

HAVE A LESSON TIME

The third part of a one-on-one meeting, the lesson time, is very important. That is where some of the building of the disciple takes place. There are eight important points to be discussed in this section of the chapter. They are first listed so that you can see where we are headed. Then we will look at each one separately.

1. Determine the possible topics that could be covered.
2. Discern the disciple's needs. (This will determine the specific topic you will want to cover.)
3. Select the material to be used.
4. Determine how you want to present the material to the disciple, and then be diligent in your preparation.
5. Summarize the principles that were learned.
6. Direct the disciple (and yourself) to specific application.
7. Emphasize accountability.
8. Seek to have the disciple's life transformed in the particular area.

To see how the three steps in the building process fit into these points, the *teaching* phase would be points one through five, *training* would cover point six, and *transforming* would be point eight. Let's examine each of these eight points.

1. DETERMINE THE POSSIBLE TOPICS THAT COULD BE COVERED

It is obvious that the goals for the disciple of maturity and multiplication cannot be realized in his life unless you think through the content you want to give him. To decide on content, you must consider goals and objectives. Both goals and objectives involve specific questions.

Goals. What do you want the disciple eventually to become? We have already answered that question. You desire that the disciple become a mature person and a spiritual multiplier.

Objectives. Objectives have to do with preparing your disciples to reach their goal, and the question here is, What knowledge must the disciples have, and what skills must they be able to master, to reach that goal?

The following pages show the goals and objectives of a discipling ministry in chart form. In the left-hand column, we have the goal and its corresponding marks written out (see chap. 3). The objectives column looks at the knowledge or skill that disciples must have to take them to the goal.

Obviously, the thirty-six objectives listed under the two goals are not exhaustive, as many other areas could be covered. Simply use the objectives list as a source of ideas for possible topics to cover in your one-on-one meetings.

Goals	Objectives
People who are mature:	1. Assurance. You want them to understand the Scripture passages dealing with assurance and security.
1. Christlike in character	2. Forgiveness. You want them to be experiencing God's love and total forgiveness. (Use Bible verses on forgiveness and confession of sin.)
2. Dependent on Christ	3. Faith. You want them to know the importance of living by faith and not feelings.
3. Independent of others	4. Holy Spirit. You want them to understand the ministry of the Holy Spirit in their lives (filling of the Spirit, walking by the Spirit, etc.).
4. Consistent in walk	5. Obedience. You want them to know the importance of living obediently.
5. Stable due to knowledge and acceptance of Bible truth	6. The Bible. You want them to have consistent times in the Bible (know the importance of the Word, how to study it, etc.).
	7. Memorization. You want them to have a system of memorizing the Scriptures.
	8. Prayer. You want them to understand the nature of prayer and begin praying consistently.
	9. Walk with God. You want them to develop their walk with God: a. Maintain consistent devotional times with God each day. b. Know how to glorify God. c. Know the nature of praise and worship.
	10. Discipline. You want them to understand the nature of God's discipline (Hebrews 12, unconfessed sin and discipline, nature of trials in our lives).
	11. Temptation. You want them to know how to deal with temptation.
	12. Stewardship. You want them to know the nature of stewardship (dealing with finances, possessions, etc.).

13. Church. You want them to know the importance of church involvement and begin regular attendance at a local church.
14. God's will. You want them to know how to discern God's will for their lives.
15. Fellowship. You want them to know their responsibilities to other Christians ("one another" commands in Scripture—love one another, encourage one another, etc.).
16. Evangelism. You want them to be effective in evangelism. (See objectives under "people who are multipliers.")
17. Biblical counseling (problem solving). You want them to know how to deal with such problems as depression, legalism, discouragement, pressure, and worry.
18. Promises. You want them to be aware of the many promises in the Bible that can be claimed.
19. Relationships. You want them to be developed in the area of relationships:
    a. with families—parents, brothers, sisters, wife, husband
    b. with friends—of the same sex and of the opposite sex
    c. with their employers and employees
20. Love. You want them to understand the biblical concept of love and begin to apply it.
21. Bible doctrine. You want them to have a basic understanding of the doctrinal truths of Christianity:
    a. doctrine of God (theology proper), attributes, the Trinity
    b. doctrine of Christ (Christology), deity of Christ
    c. doctrine of salvation (soteriology), atonement, saving faith, justification

d. doctrine of Satan and demons
e. doctrine of sin (hamartiology)
f. doctrine of last things (eschatology)
g. doctrine of Holy Spirit (pneumatology)
h. doctrine of man (anthropology)
i. doctrine of the Bible (bibliology)

22. Basic Bible knowledge. You want them to have an understanding of basic Bible knowledge such as the location of books in the Bible, themes of the books, and authorship and background.

Goals

People who are multipliers:

1. Trained in evangelism

2. Trained in grounding new Christians in the faith

3. Trained in equipping mature Christians to reproduce themselves

Objectives

1. You want them to know the importance of personal evanglism.

2. You want them to know the content of the gospel.

3. You want them to be able to communicate the gospel simply and clearly.

4. You want them to develop an evangelistic testimony.

5. You want them to have a basic knowledge of apologetics (to be able to answer questions most often asked).

6. You want them to develop an agressiveness in their evangelism (going *to* people and not waiting for people to come to them).

7. You want them to know how to make use of opportunities that arise in which they can witness (how to initiate conversations with non-Christians, how to witness on campus, at work, etc.).

8. You want them to understand the value and definition of discipling others.

9. You want them to know the goals of discipling others (men who are mature and multipliers).

10. You want them to personally catch the vision of multiplication, or spiritual reproduction.

11. You want them to know how to select and challenge potential disciples.
12. You want them to have a knowledge of the content they should teach a Christian to bring him to maturity.
13. You want them to be able to conduct a one-on-one meeting.
14. You want them to know how to build, interact with, and motivate disciples.

2. DISCERN THE DISCIPLE'S NEEDS (THIS WILL DETERMINE THE SPECIFIC TOPIC YOU WILL WANT TO COVER)

Where is the disciple in His walk with the Lord? If the disciple is a new Christian or is spiritually young, you need to cover some of the basics. If the person is somewhat mature, then other material and content should be covered.

You might ask the disciple what his immediate needs are. After he discusses his thoughts with you, determine what is a real need and what is a felt need. As I am using those terms, a real need is a need that is essential to his growth at that time. A felt need is some need that he believes he has, but which in reality is not important to his growth at that point. For example, a new Christian may say that fasting and understanding the book of Revelation are needs. As a discerning discipler, however, you understand that although those are good things, they probably are not high priorities in the "diet" of the new Christian. Pray that God would make clear to you the direction you should take.

Before leaving this point, something else needs to be mentioned. A question you might naturally have after looking at all the possible topics under "Objectives" is, Am I to personally cover each of these areas? Gary Kuhne in *The Dynamics of Personal Follow-up* has good insight in this area.[1] He says that there are three sources from which a disciple can receive information:

---

1. Gary W. Kuhne, *The Dynamics of Personal Follow-up* (Grand Rapids, Mich.: Zondervan, 1976), pp. 87-89.

from the discipler in the one-on-one meeting, from the disciple's own study, and from group teaching, such as in Bible classes and teaching from the church. It is up to you, the discipler, to determine what you will cover personally with the disciple and what the disciple will receive from the other sources.

Let's suppose you are meeting with a new Christian. If you wanted to take him through some content the first ten to twenty weeks, what subjects would you cover? Here is a suggested plan (not necessarily in the order in which they should be covered):

* assurance of salvation
* God's love and forgiveness and our confession of sin
* ministry of the Holy Spirit
* devotional time with God
* prayer
* dealing with temptation
* witnessing
* understanding God's will
* nature of faith
* importance of fellowship
* how to study the Bible
* obedience
* general survey of the Bible
* developing a personal testimony

3. SELECT THE MATERIAL TO BE USED

Some ideas for materials to use in the lesson time:

* Go through *workbooks* on Christian living.
* Go through *books* on Christian living.
* Select a *tape recording* by a speaker on the topic you choose.
* Select a *Bible passage* on the topic you choose.

4. DETERMINE HOW YOU WANT TO PRESENT THE MATERIAL TO THE DISCIPLE, AND THEN BE DILIGENT IN YOUR PREPARATION

If you are going through a workbook, you might want to present the material by having yourself and the disciple alternate in answering the questions. You might take the odd-numbered questions and the disciple the even-numbered questions. Make sure that you have answered all the questions before the meeting and are prepared to explain anything confusing to the disciple. If you are going through a Christian book, listening to a tape recording, or discussing a Bible passage, have thought questions prepared that can be discussed when you and the disciple meet. Whatever topic you choose, determine how you want to present it, and then be diligent in your preparation.

5. SUMMARIZE THE PRINCIPLES THAT WERE LEARNED

Summarize the lesson. For example, if you have just discussed Matthew 6:25-34 on why Christians should not worry, restate those principles that you have learned. You might say, "Joe, we have just gone through this passage; let's summarize what we learned. We saw that as Christians we don't have to worry because—"

6. DIRECT THE DISCIPLE (AND YOURSELF) TO SPECIFIC APPLICATION

James 1:22 says that we are to be doers of the Word and not hearers only. You need to get beyond vague generalizations as you teach and help the disciple think through what specific action he is going to take and when he is going to take it. Unfortunately, application usually becomes the weakest part of the lesson time. Many times the application is either not planned or is neglected because of lack of time. You must not let that happen. You need to ask for specific application. In a certain group, the topic being discussed was prayer; so when it came to the application time, I asked one person what he was going to do in response to the lesson. He told me that he was going to start a prayer book. I was not completely satisfied with his response. It needed to be more specific, so I asked him, "When?"

He said, "Today," and I questioned him further.

"When today?"

That sort of questioning is the kind of thing you need to do to direct the disciple and yourself to specific application.

Something else needs to be mentioned. If the learning of a skill is involved in the applying of a principle to one's life, you might want to train the disciple during the lesson time and in the following weeks. For example, during the lesson time you might have discussed a chapter or done some study on the importance of evangelism. A natural thing to do would be to train the disciple in the weeks to follow in how to witness for Christ.

7. EMPHASIZE ACCOUNTABILITY

If making specific application of principles learned from Scripture is the most often neglected step for the majority of Christians, being accountable to someone is a close second. What is accountability? It is being held responsible for one's actions. Accountability means that you have the right to question my behavior to see if I have done what I said I would do. In a discipling ministry, you and the disciple are holding each other responsible concerning the application of the principles that have been learned. Therefore, the next time you and the disciple meet, you both should discuss whether applying the principles the previous week was successful or not. Points five, six, and seven can be seen as turning specific *principles* (point five) into specific *action* (point six) with *accountability* (point seven).

8. SEEK TO HAVE THE DISCIPLE'S LIFE TRANSFORMED IN THE PARTICULAR AREA

Have the disciple do something that will promote a permanent change in his life with respect to the topic of the lesson. If, for example, the particular objective you are covering in a given week is love or compassion for others, you might have a disciple do a detailed study of Christ's compassion for the unlovely or the needy, or when reading books about Christians who reached out to the unfortunate, you might take the disciple to a convalescent home or a hospital, where he can have firsthand exposure to the needs of others. Do not forget to ask God to develop a compassionate heart in the disciple, and, of course, be a consistent example to the disciple in caring about the needs of others.

We now come to the last aspect of a one-on-one meeting. We have already looked at the opening prayer, the discussion time, and the lesson time.

CLOSE WITH CONVERSATIONAL PRAYER

In the last part of the meeting, you and your disciple might want to look at schedules with each other, that is, those activities or appointments coming up in the following week for which you desire prayer. Also, discuss with each other any other needs you might have, and do not forget to pray for each other, asking God to apply the principles you have learned. You might want to have the disciple pray first, and then you can close.

One last comment on the one-on-one meeting. Have variety in the meeting time. Do not think that you need to do the same thing each week. Here are some ideas:

Just talk and pray. One week you may not want to have a formal teaching time. Simply get together, talk about your lives, and then close in prayer for each other.

Go out and eat together. As you and the disciple eat out together you can talk informally over the meal.

Worship God together in song. Several times I have used an entire meeting to sing with the men God has given me. I take out my guitar and some song sheets, and we sing for twenty to thirty minutes, closing in prayer.

Spend the time with an older, godly individual. You might want to invite an older, godly person to spend time with the two of you to expose you to someone else's ministry and Christian walk.

Discuss a Christian book. I once gave an assignment to the men I was discipling to read a book on their own about a man who suffered because of his faith in Christ. I also read the book, and then during a meeting we discussed what we had learned.

Memorize Scripture. You would not take the time during the meeting to memorize Scripture, but you and the disciple could decide on a schedule in which the two of you would be responsible to have certain verses memorized by each meeting time. This might be done in addition to other assignments.

Whatever you do during the meeting time, make sure there is a variety and that the disciple is challenged. Once I gave all the men in my small discipling group (and myself) the assignment to read the entire New Testament, read two Christian books, memorize some Scripture, and be prepared to discuss a chapter out of a Christian book—all in one month. It was a good test of our ability to discipline ourselves.

10

MOTIVATING A DISCIPLE

Once you have begun a discipling ministry, it will not take long before you will realize that a Christian does not remain at the same level of excitement, motivation, and challenge from the day of his spiritual birth to the time of his departure. There are some low times, stagnant times, discouraging times, and dry times. The young Christian needs to be revitalized at many points in his pilgrimage, and often you will be the person the disciple will look to for help. How can you motivate him to action? What can you do to keep him from becoming stagnant or unmotivated in his Christian life? This chapter offers suggestions.

MOTIVATE THE DISCIPLE BY AN UNCONDITIONAL LOVE

In an earlier chapter we said that a discipler is to be a lover of people. You, as a discipler, ought to have a heart for people. Why is this important? Your love for the disciple will produce loyalty, commitment, and action. There is no limit to what a man can do when loved. Men were motivated to follow Christ because He loved and accepted them unconditionally. They never questioned whether He loved them.

Think about the upper room discourse in John 13-16. In those four chapters there are more exhortations to obedience than in any other four chapters in the gospels. For example, look at John 13:34; 14:15, 21, 23; and 15:10, 12, 14, 17. Yet we might ask, Was it those exhortations that motivated Jesus' disciples to obey? What approach did He use? If I were the Son of God who had the Holy Spirit without measure, and if I were sovereign and powerful, I would have said, "All right, you men, line up. I want you to know that I am leaving. And I will tell you right now that you had better watch your behavior, because when I come back, if things aren't in tip-top shape, there's going to be trouble. Now, to get things rolling, I have given Peter a list of one thousand things to do. I expect them to be finished when I return."

But was that Christ's approach? Did He motivate His disciples to action by threatening or by using His authority? No. The genius of this discourse is that interwoven through all the statements commanding them to be obedient was Christ's incredible love for them. He moved them to action by His unconditional love.

And how Christ loved His disciples! He loved them by serving them (John 13:1-5). He loved them by telling them He was preparing a place for them (John 14:1-3). He loved them by comforting them, telling them that the Holy Spirit, who was just like Him, would be in them forever (John 14:17). He loved them by warning them, in His protective love, of coming danger (John 15:18–16:4). He loved them by comforting them again (John 16:19-22), telling them that they would weep but that the same event—the cross—that caused their grief would also be a cause of rejoicing. He loved them by informing them of the privilege of prayer so that their joy could be full (John 16:23-24).

The disciples' lives are proof of the intensity of Christ's love for them. When you start conveying warmth, personal interest, concern, and acceptance, you will see things happen in the disciple's life. For practical ideas on how to show love, see the chapter on interacting with a disciple.

MOTIVATE BY ENCOURAGING THE DISCIPLE

Think of the number of times this past week that you consciously said or did something to someone else to encourage him. What do you come up with? Would you not agree that encouragement is a lost art? Yet it is so essential if disciples are to stay motivated. That is why the Bible mentions repeatedly the need for encouragement. We are to encourage one another day after day (Heb. 3:13). Paul told the Thessalonians that in addition to exhorting and imploring them, he encouraged them as a father would his own children (1 Thessalonians 2:11). He then told them to encourage and build up one another (1 Thessalonians 5:11). He told his Colossian readers that he desired that their hearts be encouraged (Colossians 2:1-2*a*), and for that reason he sent Tychicus to them (Colossians 4:8). After Paul and Silas left prison, they entered the house of Lydia and encouraged the brethren (Acts 16:40).

Encouragement is simply helping your disciple to be more God-conscious in his daily life. Why does discouragement set in? It comes because the disciple forgets that God is in control, that God is sovereign. We are all prone to dwell on the negative too much, and encouragement gives life and hope. It changes one's outlook on himself. Your words should be words of encouragement. If the disciple is going to remain steadfast in the Christian life, you have to be a master of the art of encouragement. Encouragement is not catering to one's ego but causing a person to become more Christ-conscious.

What are some practical ways of encouraging a disciple? A few ideas are given below.

EXPRESS ENCOURAGING THOUGHTS TO HIM

We are so quick to *think* encouraging things about someone else, yet so slow to express those thoughts. How often it is that we think about a person and realize how much we appreciate him, yet never *tell him* of our appreciation. The apostle Paul was not like that. He was quick to put his thoughts of appreciation into words that encouraged the hearts of his readers. But what can you tell the disciple?

Tell the disciple about the joy he brings to you. A young Christian may often think that his life is of no value. The disciple needs to know that he is important to you. When he becomes a joy to you, let him know. It will encourage him. Again, we see this in Paul. He told the Thessalonians, "For who is our hope or joy or crown of exultation? Is it not even you, in the presence of our Lord Jesus at His coming? For you are our glory and joy" (1 Thessalonians 2:19-20). What encouraging words! Suppose someone said that to you? Wouldn't you be motivated?

Tell the disciple that you notice his growth in Christ. Point out changes you have seen in the disciple's life as he grows in Christ. Point out the impact he has had in others' lives. If you are like me, you tend to overlook the positive changes God is working in your life and dwell on the sins with which you are struggling.

The disciple is the same way. He needs to know that God is indeed alive and well in his life. This is one of my favorite ways of encouraging. When a disciple sees that God has changed him and is working in his life, it gives him hope for conquering the sins with which he is struggling. Here are just two examples of this kind of encouragement from the apostle Paul. Many more can be found in his epistles.

> We ought always to give thanks to God for you, brethren, as is only fitting, because your faith is greatly enlarged, and the love of each one of you toward one another grows ever greater; therefore, we ourselves speak proudly of you among the churches of God for your perseverance and faith in the midst of all your persecutions and afflictions which you endure. (2 Thessalonians 1:3-4)

> For the word of the Lord has sounded forth from you, not only in Macedonia and Achaia, but also in every place your faith toward God has gone forth, so that we have no need to say anything. (1 Thessalonians 1:8)

Tell the disciple about those positive qualities that others notice in him. Listen to the comments that others make about the person you are discipling. Take note of things mentioned, and then relay them to the disciple. One of the men I discipled went to Yosemite National Park and had a chance to witness to several people. He was so fervent in his evangelism that a Christian who was with him said to me. "He was such an example to me in evangelism. It was convicting, watching him." You can be sure that the next time I saw that brother, I told him what the other person said about him. Was he ever encouraged!

Look at Paul's statement to Philemon: "I thank my God always, making mention of you in my prayers, because *I hear of your love, and of the faith which you have toward the Lord Jesus, and toward all the saints"* (Philemon 4-5; emphasis added). Now Paul could have simply kept that knowledge of Philemon's life to himself, but he did not. He told Philemon what he had heard other people say. So listen to the comments of others concerning the disciple, and then relate those comments to him.

Tell the disciple how he ministers to you. As the young Christian grows, he will begin to manifest Christ in his life in a unique way. You will see qualities in the disciple's life that will be a motivation for your own. When that happens—when the disciple has that effect—tell him. A young Christian can think that he has nothing to offer to an older, more mature Christian. But when he is told that his life is an example to you in a specific area, his desire for growth will be strengthened. One man I discipled is an example to me in his disciplined study of the Word. Another exhibits the qualities of humility, honesty, and teachability. Another ministers to me in his sensitivity to the needs of others, and another exhibits the gift of helps, a willingness to give of himself to meet others' needs. Each man has been used by God to influence my life and change me. I have told each one how God has used him to minister to me.

SEND THE DISCIPLE NOTES OF APPRECIATION

Encouragement is contagious. One week I received two notes from people who were expressing their appreciation of me. I was so uplifted and encouraged that I had to write someone else a note, telling him how much he meant to me. Once in a while, send the disciple a note in the mail. Tell him how much you appreciate him.

WHEN YOU ARE PRAYING WITH THE DISCIPLE, MENTION HIM BY NAME AND THANK GOD FOR HIM

It is to be hoped that it will be natural for you to thank God for the disciple. So thank God for him when he can hear it. When the disciple hears that he is a reason for your thanksgiving to God in your prayers, it will encourage him.

BE INTERESTED AND EXCITED OVER WHAT THE DISCIPLE IS DOING

Take an interest in the disciple's activities. Perhaps he had an opportunity to witness to someone at school or work and is jumping up and down, excitedly telling you how God gave him the boldness to open his mouth. What should be your response? You, too, jump up and down. "Rejoice with those who rejoice" (Romans 12:15). Nothing will dampen the disciple's enthusiasm more than for you to say, "Fine. Now listen to the five opportunities I had today."

Or suppose the disciple discovers a spiritual truth in his study of the Word. He comes to you saying, "You will never guess what God just taught me from the Word. It is exciting! I have never seen that before!" How should you respond?

"You mean it took you this long to discover that simple truth?"

I guarantee that if that is your response the disciple will never again become excited in your presence about truths he has learned from the Bible.

Be interested in all that the disciple does. If he is involved in some project, outreach, or activity, ask him questions. Show concern. Let him know that you share his excitement and enthusiasm.

MOTIVATE BY CHALLENGING THE DISCIPLE TO GREATER FAITH

A disciple who is not being challenged continually to greater faith in his God is probably an unmotivated disciple. When a person is asked to trust God in a new area of life, you might say that all his spiritual faculties are energized. For example, his prayer life is rekindled. Trust in God usually brings with it bended knees. When a person is challenged to greater faith, his sense of need for God is heightened. He is also motivated to live a holy life. When he has to trust God, he is motivated to make sure that his life is blameless. There is a seriousness in dealing with sin when he is challenged to greater faith. But how can you stretch the disciple's faith?

GIVE THE DISCIPLE RESPONSIBILITY, AND THEN INCREASE IT ACCORDING TO HIS RESPONSE

Giving the disciple responsibility is the primary way to challenge him to greater faith. You need to guide the disciple into increasing responsibilities. You need to give him tasks to perform. Involvement always brings about motivation. Jesus was the master of this, as He continually had something for the disciples to do. For example, in John 4:2, the disciples were engaged in the task of baptizing; in John 6:1-13, they were distributing baskets of food; and in John 21:15, Peter was given the responsibility to feed Christ's lambs.

I once went with a group of Christians to a rest home where

older people live. We were to put on a Christmas program for them. In addition to a short message, we decided that a personal testimony by one member of the group would be a good idea. So I approached one of the men I was discipling and asked him to consider giving his testimony. Terror gripped him! He asked me why he was chosen, and I told him that we thought he could do a good job. You should have seen him. He was breathing faster, his heart was beating quicker, and he was in a daze. He had never done anything like that before, and he was not eager to do it. After we talked for a few minutes, he said, "Allen, I'm going to do it." I have never seen anyone more motivated in his Christian life than that young man was in the next two weeks. His personal times with the Lord were consistent and rich. His prayer life was deepened. He practiced his testimony numerous times. He memorized it frontward and backward. He was sensitive to sin as he had never been before. Why all the changes? Responsibility motivated him into action.

A footnote to this is that fulfilled responsibility also increases motivation because of the success, or victory, factor. In Luke 10, Jesus is giving His disciples instruction before sending them out. I doubt they were particularly motivated when they heard Him say, "Go your ways; behold, I send you out as lambs in the midst of wolves" (Luke 10:3). But they returned from their mission with great joy. Why? Because they had experienced success. "And the seventy returned with joy, saying, 'Lord, even the demons are subject to us in Your name' " (Luke 10:17). They saw God use them in ways they had not seen before, and it brought joy and motivation to them.

The same was true with the disciple who shared his testimony. After it was over, he was a joyous person. God had used him. His faith was stretched. He had seen victory.

One reason many Christians are not motivated in the Christian life is because they have no victories in the Lord. The reason there are no victories is that they do not place themselves in situations in which they have to trust God to give them victory. Christians tend to play it safe, and thus they do not step out in new areas of responsibility. The result is a stagnant life-style. It is your responsibility as a discipler to kick the disciples out of the nest, give them responsibility, and expose them to situations in which their faith will be tested.

Give them responsibility, and then increase it as they demonstrate the willingness and ability to handle it. You might place a disciple in charge of some ministry or project or have him give his testimony somewhere. You might have him lead one of the discipling-group lessons. Be creative. This is a highly challenging area for you, the discipler, to tackle. Do not give the disciple the chance to remain static in his faith.

HAVE THE DISCIPLE READ BOOKS THAT SHOW HOW MEN OF GOD TRUST GOD

Reading biographical or autobiographical books on men of God never ceases to be a challenge and motivation to me in my spiritual life. For example, after reading Brother Andrew's book *God's Smuggler*, I said, "Lord, challenge my faith the way You challenged Brother Andrew's." I was so motivated to trust God in my life that I actually wanted God to put me in situations in which I had to trust Him. And God was faithful. There are so many books on men of God. Have your disciple read about David Brainerd, George Müller, Henry Martyn, Dawson Trotman, Billy Graham, or Hudson Taylor. Without a doubt, the lives of those men will challenge the disciple to greater faith.

HAVE THE DISCIPLE READ ABOUT MEN OF FAITH IN THE BIBLE

Direct the disciple's attention to men like Jesus, Paul, Daniel, Joseph, Abraham, and Moses. What an encouragement the lives of those men will be to him.

HAND THE DISCIPLE PERSONAL CHALLENGES

Some time ago, I gave the men I was discipling one challenge per week. I called it "Allen's Challenge." It consisted of exhortations to Christian living that came either from me or from something I found in a book. Those brief messages were designed to stimulate the disciples to commitment and greater faith. This is an example of one of my challenges:

ALLEN'S CHALLENGE

Many Christians felt strongly rebuked when Billy Graham first read publicly the following letter, written by an American college student who had been converted to Communism in Mexico. The purpose of the letter was to explain to his fiancée why he had to break off their engagement:

"We Communists have a high casualty rate. We're the ones who get shot and hung and lynched and tarred and feathered and jailed and slandered, and ridiculed and fired from our jobs, and in every other way made as uncomfortable as possible. A certain pecentage of us get killed or imprisoned. We live in virtual poverty. We turn back to the party every penny we make above what is absolutely necessary to keep us alive. We Communists don't have the time or the money for many movies, or concerts, or T-bone steaks, or decent homes and new cars. We've been described as fanatics. We are fanatics. Our lives are dominated by one great overshadowing factor, *the struggle for world Communism.*

"We Communists have a philosophy of life which no amount of money could buy. We have a cause to fight for, a definite purpose in life. We subordinate our petty, personal selves into a great movement of humanity, and if our personal lives seem hard, or our egos appear to suffer through subordination to the party, then we are adequately compensated by the thought that each of us in his small way is contributing to something new and true and better for mankind. There is one thing in which I am in dead earnest and that is the communist cause. It is my life, my business, my religion, my hobby, my sweetheart, my wife and mistress, my bread and meat. I work at it in the daytime and dream of it at night. Its hold on me grows, not lessens as times goes on. Therefore, I cannot carry on a friendship, a love affair, or even a conversation without relating it to this force which both drives and guides my life. I evaluate people, books, ideas and actions according to how they affect the Communist cause and by their attitude toward it. I've already been in jail because of my ideas and if necessary, I'm ready to go before a firing squad."

If Communists can be as dedicated as this to their cause, how much more should Christians pour themselves out in loving, glad devotion to their glorious Lord. Surely if the Lord Jesus is worth anything, He is worth everything.[1]

MOTIVATE BY CONVEYING ENTHUSIASM

I am so glad that when I became a Christian, I was with Christians who were excited about the Christian life. From the

1. William MacDonald, *True Discipleship* (Kansas City: Walterick, 1962), pp. 28-29.

very beginning of my spiritual life, I caught a positive perspective on what the Christian life is all about. That positive perspective really has been all that I have known. I was with people who were enthusiastic about serving God, trusting God, obeying God, witnessing for God, and being used by God. You can imagine how motivated I was. Because of the impact those people had on me, I can say that the Christian life is very exciting.

Motivate the disciple by enthusiasm. What exactly is enthusiasm? Someone defined it as "an intense emotion of zeal toward a purposeful goal or meaningful action." It involves a Spirit-filled, optimistic, joyful, positive attitude that naturally draws others to similar goals or actions.

I once met a young man on a college campus every Wednesday at 1:00 o'clock. I would come to him and discuss with him the events of that day. I would say to him, "You'll never guess what happened. I talked to a student this morning who was so open to the gospel. What a great conversation we had!" The next week I met him and said to him, "What a morning. I talked to a young man earlier, and he had every kind of argument and question concerning Christianity. What a discussion we had! We talked for one and a half hours. You should have been there." I did this every week.

Do you know what eventually happened? My enthusiasm for witnessing rubbed off on that fellow. Telling him those stories created a desire in him to witness for Christ. He finally said to me one day, "Allen, when are you going to take me with you as you share your faith?" It was not my cramming down his throat Scripture on the Christian's duty to witness that got him excited, but rather an enthusiastic life-style.

I often stop and evaluate my life, taking note of the presence or lack of enthusiasm in it. What kind of perspective on the Christian life are my disciples forming? It will probably be the one I am communicating to them. What about you? Are disciples motivated in living the Christian life because of your enthusiasm?

MOTIVATE BY A CONSISTENT WALK

The consistent, godly life of mature saints had a very positive effect on my early Christian life. As a young Christian, I would look at people who had been Christians longer than I had and say, "Lord, I want to be like that." I was intensely motivated to pattern my life after theirs. That is what a consistent walk will do. Gary Kuhne comments on this effect of a consistent life:

> I thought that seeing how mature I was would tend to discourage [my disciples] as they saw how far they needed to come. This obviously didn't happen. I think there are two reasons for this. First, I have never reached a level of maturity that awed people into defeat (does anyone?). Secondly, maturity actually does motivate. In my own experience, the opportunities to spend time with a real saint of the faith most motivated me to seek to mature in my own life.[2]

The same will be true of those you disciple. As they observe your godly, consistent walk, they will be motivated to follow you and thus Christ.

MOTIVATE BY SEEING THE POTENTIAL OF THE DISCIPLE

You must believe that God can make those you disciple into significant ambassadors in His Kingdom. Every person has significance. But unless you see that potential in the disciples, you will not be able to motivate them to do anything. Why? Because the way you perceive them determines how they will function. You need to see them for what they can become, not just for what they are now.

Jesus always saw potential in His men. In John 17:20 He did not pray, "Father, I know these disciples will fail, but I ask that You will raise up a new batch who will spread Your Word." No. He told His Father that He was praying for "those ... who believe in Me through *their word*" (emphasis added). What foresight! Prior to Pentecost, I certainly would not have made a statement like that. I would have felt as if I were presuming on God to believe that the disciples would spread the Word and have such an impact that others would believe. Yet Jesus looked past the disciples to the third generation. He saw potential.

How does seeing the potential in the disciple motivate him? Once you believe that God can make the disciple into a signifi-

2. Gary W. Kuhne, *The Dynamics of Personal Follow-up* (Grand Rapids, Mich.: Zondervan, 1976), p. 117.

cant person, you need to communicate the potential that you see in him. Give him a purpose for his life. Continually put the purpose before him. The specific purpose I am referring to is to be a spiritual multiplier. Tell the disciple that God wants to use him in a meaningful way in the lives of other people.

I will never forget the first few times I met with one individual whom I discipled several years ago. He was a very young Christian, and when I first began meeting with him, I had my doubts about the impact he would have in other people's lives. But I discussed the "picture of multiplication" with him (see chap. 3) and pointed out to him that eventually he would be discipling other young men. I told him that in time God would be using him to reach others for Christ and then build them up in the faith. It was difficult for him to see that taking place in his life. But I planted the seed, and it established in his mind from the very beginning of our relationship that God wanted to use him in the lives of others. And sure enough, after a while he got involved in a discipling ministry.

One thing I do regularly in discipling is to plant the seed-thought of purpose in the minds of the men. I accomplish that in several ways. I do it when I am praying with them. I say something like this: "Thank You, Lord, that someday John will have the privilege of pouring his life into someone else." I also seize those opportunities when a disciple expresses his appreciation for my helping him in his growth. I respond to his statement of appreciation by telling him, "I know that someday the Lord will give *you* men that *you* can help grow closer to Christ. I do not want my care to stop with you. Someday you will have the chance to pass it on to other young men, just as I have done to you." Planting that prospect in the disciple's mind will broaden his perspective of the Christian life and give him a sense of purpose that will lead to a motivated life.

MOTIVATE BY EMPHASIZING PRACTICAL TRAINING

One of the most significant reasons many disciples are not motivated to action in the Christian life is that no one has taken the time to show them *how* to develop a particular skill. For example, when I learned *how* to witness for Christ to others, I was motivated to witness. When I learned *how* to study the Bible, no one could stop me from studying it. When I learned *how* to disciple others, I was motivated to disciple others. There are many frustrated Christians who desire to grow in their walk with Christ but who remain in neutral because they have not been trained in a particular skill. All they need is for someone to show them the way, someone to give them direction. You can be critical of disciples because of their inconsistency in studying the Word or their lack of zeal in witnessing to others. Yet it may be that their problem can be tied to a lack of direction on your part in teaching them the skills and then perfecting their skills. If you want to motivate them "show them how."

MOTIVATE BY PRAYING FOR THE DISCIPLE

Spiritual growth is the result of the blending together of human and divine elements. From the discipler's perspective, prayer releases the divine factor, the ministry of the Holy Spirit, into the disciple's life. Paul certainly realized that. Imagine continually praying to God for a disciple in the following manner:

> We have not ceased to pray for you and to ask that you may be filled with the knowledge of His will in all spiritual wisdom and understanding, so that you may walk in a manner worthy of the Lord, to please Him in all respects, bearing fruit in every good work and increasing in the knowledge of God. (Colossians 1:9-10)

What was Paul's goal for the Colossians? It was that they walk in a manner worthy of the Lord, pleasing Him and bearing fruit. What was his method for getting them there? He prayed for them. Look also at Philippians 1:9-10:

> And this I pray, that your love may abound still more and more in real knowledge and all discernment, so that you may approve the things that are excellent, in order to be sincere and blameless until the day of Christ.

Again, Paul's desire was for blamelessness on the part of the Philippians. What was his method? Prayer. If you want to see disciples reaching biblical goals, prayer has to be the foundation of your ministry. Let's face it, prayer is mysterious and we are not always sure how it works, but we do know that God honors our prayers.

MOTIVATE BY GETTING THE DISCIPLE INTO THE BIBLE

How effective is the Bible in motivating people? Think back in your life to those times when God used specific verses or passages to challenge you to a godly walk. What about those times when the Word encouraged you to remain steadfast or comforted you? One of the most meaningful times I have had in the Word was when I read Psalm 119 in one sitting. You cannot read the chapter without getting the overpowering feeling that that psalmist had an attitude toward the Word that few have matched. The Word was his delight (v. 77) and love (v. 48). It kept him from sin (v. 11), counseled him (v. 24), produced reverence for God (v. 38), increased his wisdom (v. 98), guided his steps (v. 105), gave him peace (v. 165), and gave him understanding (v. 104).

Because the power of the Word endures forever, that same life-changing experience of the psalmist can also be ours. One of the most significant things you can do for disciples is to teach them how to study the Bible. After all, the Bible tells us God's unconditional love for us, encourages us, increases our faith, and reveals for our instruction men who were enthusiastic concerning their God and who were consistent examples. The Word also provides many examples of men who, although failures at first, were greatly used by God. And the Word gives us things for which to pray concerning those we disciple.

11
THE SMALL DISCIPLING GROUP—
Part One

In chapter 6, entitled "Selecting and Challenging Potential Disciples," it was noted that there are two possible formats in a discipling ministry, the one-on-one relationship and the small group. Although the emphasis of this book has been on the one-on-one relationship, there may come a time in your discipling ministry when you would like to start a small discipling group. Because of that possibility, it is important that we devote a few pages to a discussion of the small discipling group. As we examine this area, we will be looking at four topics:

- the value of a group
- the people in the group
- the challenge to a group
- the conducting of a group meeting

VALUE OF A GROUP

When comparing the one-on-one relationship with the small discipling group, it becomes apparent that each of the two formats has its benefits. In fact, the ideal discipling situation would be to have the disciple involved in a small group with other Christians and also meeting one-on-one with you. For example, the one-on-one meeting gives you the opportunity to really get to know the person. It allows the disciple to ask questions and discuss personal problems. It gives you the opportunity to personally exhort and encourage him. And, of course, if you are beginning a discipling ministry, a one-on-one meeting is not as difficult as a small-group situation.

What are some of the benefits of having a small discipling group? First, it provides those in the group with an opportunity for close fellowship with more than one person. Second, friendships are developed.

The first two benefits are closely related. As one has fellowship with others through the sharing of burdens and joys and growing together, friendships are built. One individual wrote this prayer to the Lord, expressing his gratitude for the other men in his group:

Dear Father,

I just want to take this time to say that since I've become a Christian, You've blessed my life in so many ways that I can't thank You ever as much as is due to You. You've filled my life with such wonderful brothers. They are such an inspiration to me in my walk with You that I can't help but think of You and Your never-ending love and efforts to fill all the needs that we have.

Another said in his prayer, "Thanks, Lord, that I can wake up each morning, knowing I have friends who love me. Thank You that I don't have to stay home alone, but You've given me friends to do things with."

Another person said, "Allen, a few months ago I was told by a friend that I had come to a point where I needed to commit [a second friend] into God's hands. Back then I couldn't do it, but now I'm able to because I realize that God has filled the void in my life through the love of all the guys."

If you start a group, you will find that in time the main reasons the disciples will want to come are the twofold benefits of fellowship and friendship.

A third benefit of a small group is that it provides the disciple with an emotional home where he is accepted. Many times, a disciple does not feel loved or accepted by those at home, at work, or by some of his friends. In a discipling group, in which it is to be hoped that the love of Christ is present, the disciple will be accepted by the other people in the group. He will begin to see that meeting time as an opportunity to discuss openly his struggles and joys, because he knows he will be listened to and cared for.

Fourth, the small discipling group provides the members with an opportunity to develop a sensitivity to others. In a group context, you are always aware of the needs of the others in the group, and that awareness builds a "reaching out" attitude and a loving concern.

Finally, the small discipling group gives the disciple greater exposure to God's personal working in people's lives. As he hears of the ways God is causing the others to grow, the disciple will be able to identify with some of the others in the group whose walks parallel his own. That will encourage him as he seeks to trust God in his life.

PEOPLE IN THE GROUP

As you consider starting a group, you have to determine the kinds of people who will be involved in it. The question to ask yourself is whether you will challenge only people at the same level of maturity or whether you will challenge people at different levels of maturity. In other words, will the group be composed of individuals who are at similar or different levels of spiritual development?

There are obvious benefits to both kinds of groups. A group composed of people at the same level of maturity will promote a balance in the interaction during the meeting. A person who is obviously more mature could easily dominate the discussion. A second benefit is that all the members will be able to identify with the others in the group because there will be a similarity in the problems and struggles experienced. A third benefit concerns the discipler's preparation for the lesson time. It is difficult to "feed" people at two levels of maturity. To which level will you direct the lesson?

A group composed of people at different levels also has its advantages. For example, the more mature individual could stimulate the others to grow. He could be a resource person and another model to the young Christians. Having a more mature individual in the group would also help the less mature believers to see that there are levels of progression in growth. It is to be hoped that the realization that growth is progressive will motivate the less mature believer to desire to grow in Christ. Another benefit of having a more mature person in the group is that you, as the leader, can view the group as a training time for the mature Christian. You can have him lead the group once in a while, and you can also encourage some of the others in the group to seek his counsel on areas in their lives.

Those are a few advantages to having individuals at the same or different levels of maturity in a group. You simply have to decide which way to go and, of course, how the Lord leads you in your particular situation.

CHALLENGE TO A GROUP

Just as you challenge someone to meet with you in a one-on-one relationship, a similar challenge is needed when beginning a group. Here is a sample challenge:

George, I want to tell you about something and ask that you pray about your possible involvement. God has been leading me to start a small discipling group, and I am looking for people who have a heart for God and a real desire to learn and grow in Christ. That is why I am telling you this—because I see in your life that desire to be all that God wants you to be. The goals of the group are twofold: that each of us grows to maturity in Christ; and second, that we learn to reproduce ourselves in others through evangelism and discipling. I am personally excited about leading such a group, because I know lives will be changed as we meet together, learn material, discuss our lives, develop friendships, and gain a purpose for our lives. As I said, I am looking for people who have a heart for God, a teachable spirit, and also a sense of faithfulness. The time commitment would involve one to two hours a week, meeting in a group itself and also meeting one-on-one with me. Would you pray about this and see if God would have you to be involved?

CONDUCTING A GROUP MEETING

Conducting the actual group meeting is very similar to the one-on-one meeting because four elements are common to both meetings—opening prayer, discussion time, study time, and conversational prayer. However, there is one big difference in the lesson, or study, time. After you have determined the topic and have selected the material to be used in a small-group meeting, use the guided discussion approach as the method for presenting the material. This will mean that you will have to prepare discussion questions that are based on the material you told them to read the previous week. As you ask those questions, the key principles of the material will be mentioned, and you will be able to direct your disciples to specific application.

The next chapter will cover in more detail the formulating

and directing of questions. The following material under "Using the Guided Discussion Method" is reprinted from a Campus Crusade for Christ staff manual.[1]

USING THE GUIDED DISCUSSION METHOD

a. *Recognize the advantages of the guided discussion.*
(1) It is the best method for creating leadership abilities.
(2) It draws out the potential of those in the class.
(3) It produces people with well-thought-through personal convictions.
(4) It builds self-confidence.
(5) It helps students learn to express themselves clearly.
(6) It allows for maximum student participation, which results in increased motivation.
(7) Students will be motivated to further thought, investigation and personal interaction on the issues discussed.
(8) It forces students to think through concepts that have been hazy to them.
(9) It helps them be open to new ideas because the students realize they are forming their own conclusions rather than having the conclusions of someone else forced on them against their will, as they sometimes feel with more structured methods.
(10) The informality allows the teacher and students to know what the other members of the group really think and what they feel, thus giving them an opportunity to help others with their personal needs.

b. *Recognize the advantages for the leader of the guided discussion group.*
(1) It does not require a leader with great public speaking ability in order to be successful.
(2) It allows for flexibility.
(3) Because of the small size of the group and the interaction, it enables the teacher to better determine whether the students are really learning or not.

1. *Campus Ministry Manual*, Campus Ministry, Campus Crusade for Christ, Inc., Arrowhead Springs, San Bernardino, CA. 92414, pp. 329-34. Printed by permission. Copyright © Campus Crusade for Christ, Inc. (1974) All rights reserved.

c. *Consider the limitations of the guided discussion method.*
   (1) It is not the place to present a large volume of content. It is used instead when it is important for the students to think through the issues.
   (2) It should only be used when preceded by preparation common to all the students.
   (3) It requires a thorough background on the part of the leader.

d. *Avoid the following pitfalls in your guided discussion.*
   (1) Don't forget that the teacher and students may not feel the need for personal preparation because they may feel that they can cover up their lack of preparation in the discussion. However, the success of a good guided discussion depends on the thorough preparation of both students and instructor. Without proper preparation on the part of the students, it will become a pooling of ignorance.
   (2) Keep in mind that it is sometimes difficult to get a good discussion started. Without proper guidance a few people may monopolize the discussion, and others may tend not to become involved. It may lead to argument. This is not bad if the proper attitudes are maintained in the disagreement. There may be a tendency for the teacher to talk too much. There may be a tendency for the inexperienced teacher to correct the students and to present his own conclusions rather than let the group come to these conclusions on their own. Such a tendency will inhibit the discussion and will nullify the advantages of the guided discussion.
   (3) Remember, it is possible to get off on unfruitful tangents. There may be a tendency for the inexperienced teacher to let the discussion drift away from the purpose of the particular session. There may be a tendency for students to reach conclusions without making *applications* to their personal lives and ministry.

e. *Prepare for the guided discussion.*
   (1) Clealy assign ahead of time the student preparation, communicating that it should be completed before the time of the discussion.

(2) Assign the students to study and follow any instructions contained in the printed syllabus.

(3) In giving an assignment of necessary reading, keep the volume of reading to a bare minimum. The purpose is to allow the student to do the maximum preparation in the minimum of time.

(4) Make certain that the syllabus contains all of the material to be read or indicate to the student where the material to be studied can be found. (If there are references to reading material outside of the syllabus, this material must be readily available to all the students so that all of them can complete the preparations before meeting time.)

(5) Provide the student with questions concerning the reading so that he will read with a purpose in mind and thus will be better prepared for the discussion.

(6) Have in mind ahead of time *what [you are] seeking to accomplish* in the particular discussion session. [You] must be very well prepared for the discussion. It takes much more background preparation than does a lecture. Acting as though he were preparing to give a *lecture,* the teacher should prepare a *logical framework, limiting himself to communicate approximately three main points.* The aim is to get those present to do the talking, to say essentially what the teacher would have said had he been giving them a lecture.

f. *Conduct the guided discussion.*

(1) [Get] the discussion started.

Begin class with an opening statement (4-10 minutes) briefly outlining the subject to be discussed, a series of agree-disagree questions or some other "hook." . . . This opening statement should be a summary of the ideas contained in the syllabus and in the homework assignment. Mention the topic or idea that you would like to have them discuss.

(2) [Begin the] discussion.

Call upon the most talkative students. Once the members are used to one another, this is not necessary.

When the talkative ones have talked long enough, bring others into the discussion.

(3) [Keep] the discussion going.

By watching the faces of the students you can tell who would like to participate in the discussion. You should be watching reactions, both vocal and silent, of all the members in the group in order to ascertain the feeling of each individual. It is your responsibility to keep the discussion from getting off on unfruitful tangents. When the discussion does get off on an unprofitable tangent, you must tactfully direct the discussion back to the major issue at hand. (Quickly!!)

(4) Unobtrusively guide the discussion by switching from one speaker to another and by putting in a word here and there of your own. You should see that no one monopolizes the discussion. You may suggest that some other person give his opinion or reaction. If necessary, you may ask the person monopolizing the conversation to give the other people an opportunity to express themselves. This may be done in public during the discussion or in private before subsequent discussions.

(5) See that everyone is involved in the discussion. You should feel free to call upon those who don't volunteer to become involved. You should counsel in private, encouraging the more quiet members to be more vocal in the discussion. *You should personally enter the discussion as little as possible.* The leader plays a very important role in the discussion even though he does not say much.

(6) [Ask] appropriate questions.

Characteristics of good questions:

Questions should be *brief* and *simple*. The pupil should be able to grasp the meaning quickly. Questions should be clear, with only one possible interpretation as to what is meant. This demands great care in the choice of words and phrasing of sentences.

(7) Provoke thought and test judgment, not merely the memory, through questions. Questions should never suggest the answer. Questions should not offer the

student a choice between two possible answers contained in the question because that does not compel the student to think, but rather to guess. Avoid questions with only a "yes" or "no" answer.

(8) Adapt questions to the knowledge and experience of the pupil giving special attention to the quickest and slowest in the group and providing each an opportunity to answer. Questions should prepare the person for further study, starting a train of associated ideas. Questions should be logical and interrelated. Questions should fulfill an essential purpose and not merely be asked for the sake of asking. Questions should be asked in a conversational, spontaneous way, as if personally addressed to each of the group before one is selected to answer. Questions should keep in mind the end result of personal application.

(9) Techniques of questioning:
Questions should be asked in an informal way, implying that the student is able to answer.
Questions should be distributed so that all have an opportunity to learn as nearly equally as possible. This should not involve a purely mechanical distribution, e.g., alphabetically, seating order, etc. Strike a balance between calling on volunteers and stimulating shy people.

(10) Allow sufficient time for a person to answer. Do not be impatient. Pacing questions too rapidly with insufficient time to answer them will distract rather than develop the thinking skill. The answer should not be suggested by word, hint, inflection of voice, or in any other way. The leader should systematize and integrate his questioning process to provide a unity and coherence which will lead the class through the material in an organized way.

(11) Preparation for questioning:
Have a *written plan* for the guided discussion. [The leader] should *think through the logical framework* he has prepared with its main points he hopes to communicate to the class. He should thoroughly study the mate-

rial which the students have studied in preparation for the discussion. He should *write out in advance* questions for discussion that would lead the students step-by-step from the material they have studied to the points he wants them to think through and accept.

(12) Plan questions that will challenge the thinking of the students and cause them to think through issues they possibly have not thought through before. [You] should always be ready with general questions that will stimulate and guide thinking. The following are examples: Do the rest of you agree? What do you think this means? Can anyone else think of any more ideas along this line? What can we learn from this? How does this apply to your daily life? What is the relationship between these ideas?

g. *Proceed step-by-step through the outline.*

(1) Seek to get *each* class member to talk on *each* major point of the outline. It is important that each person come to his own conclusions through study and discussion rather than feel that conclusions are being forced upon him. You should seek to see that everyone basically agrees on the main conclusion reached before moving the discussion on to the next major point.

(2) When the group is in basic agreement on a conclusion, simply see that the discussion moves on to the next point, rather than saying something like, "Yes, that is right, I agree, let's move on." The conclusions should be the conclusions of the students and they should feel that the conclusions are theirs.

h. *Deal with problems.*

(1) If an obviously wrong conclusion is reached by someone, let the other members of the group correct the conclusion. A student will take correction by other students much more readily than he will from you. If the other members of the group do not voluntarily correct the wrong conclusion, you should not correct it. Simply ask the group what they feel about the matter and thus allow them to express their ideas and correct the wrong conclusion.

(2) If a person is not in agreement with the basic conclusion that the group collectively is reaching, remember, he often will be silent. You may casually suggest that since he has not expressed a point of view, he may have some doubts or difficulties with what the group has collectively concluded. Suggest that if he does, he might like to express his doubts or difficulties so that the group may collectively help him solve the problem.

i. *Reach conclusions.*

(1) *At appropriate points* and *at the conclusion*, summarize the major conclusions that have been reached by the group. It is your responsibility to *help objectify conclusions that are reached.* You may do this by saying: "Is everyone generally agreed that such and such is correct? If so, let's move on to such and such idea."

(2) Making application.

Encourage students to make applications at appropriate times during the discussion. *Conclude* the discussion time by having members share how they are going to apply what they have discussed or how they have applied it during the week. Begin a subsequent action group by having students share how they have made applications to their lives as a result of previous discussions.

j. *Evaluate and improve the guided discussion.*

(1) Soon after a guided discussion, make a written evaluation of the discussion time. List the good points and the bad points. Think through how you could have handled it differently to have improved it. Utilize your evaluations to help you do a better job the next time you have a discussion.

(2) Talk with the students and make sure that they are really learning from the sessions what you think they are learning. At appropriate times have other students and staff help you make your evaluations.

After the meeting has taken place, it is wise to evaluate the time. Here is a series of questions you can ask yourself. The following material is reprinted from a Campus Crusade for Christ staff manual.[2]

1. Was everyone at the meeting who should have been there? What do you need to do to contact anyone who was absent?
2. Did you begin and end on time? What do you need to do to improve on this?
3. Were you thoroughly prepared for the session? What would enable you to be better prepared for subsequent sessions?
4. What was your objective for this particular session? Was it reached in each person's life? Why or why not?
5. Did everyone participate in the discussion? Did certain people tend to dominate or to be left out of the discussion? What can be done to produce a better balance?
6. Did people open up to share or did you have to carry the discussion? Were you able to draw the correct answers out of the group rather than giving them the answers? What could be done to improve this?
7. Did the group get off on unprofitable tangents? How can you better keep the discussion on target?
8. Was the discussion theoretical or was it practical and related to the lives of the people involved? How could you have better related it to practical Christian living?
9. Did everyone reach the desired conclusion, or did some go away with unresolved questions? Are there people in the group that you should meet with for personal counsel before the next session?
10. What other suggestions can you make that will enable you to do a better job in your next session?

12

THE SMALL DISCIPLING GROUP—
Part Two

For effective interaction in a small group, prepare discussion questions based on the material the group was assigned to read. Two important areas need to be considered in developing appropriate questions:

WHAT KINDS OF QUESTIONS SHOULD I FORMULATE?

Three kinds of questions can be formulated. The first is the *content* question. This asks the group to answer a question that is directing them to specific content in the material they read. They are parroting back information discussed by the author. Examples of this kind of question are, "What are the three keys to Christian living mentioned in the chapter we read this past week?" or, "What did the author say would happen if a Christian doesn't confess sin?" These questions lay an excellent foundation for the second type of questions that can be formulated, the *thought* questions.

Thought questions ask the members of the group to think through the implications of the material presented by the author. You are asking them not to parrot back the information given (content questions) but to *think* for themselves. A thought question can take several forms. One asks to summarize the contents of the chapter in a single sentence. This forces the discipling group to think for themselves what the central thrust was. Another is to ask them to explain why they think what the author said was important. A third is to give them agree/disagree statements. Again this forces them to think and state their reasons for agreeing or disagreeing with the author's position.

Still another method is to ask them how a principle they learned relates to another area of Christian living. For example, you have just read material on the importance of prayer, but now you want the group to think through how the prayers of believers relate to the sovereignty of God. Any way you can stimulate them to *think through* for themselves the material presented, it will serve the purpose of this kind of question.

After you have given *content* and *thought* questions, you're now ready for *application* questions. These help the members of the group to consider what they will do to put into practice the principles learned. For example, you may ask, "What is one thing you'd like to do this week in light of what you have learned?" Remember, you're asking not for a vague answer but for a specific life response. The issue isn't, "What *should* we do about what we've learned?" but rather, "What *will* we do about what we've learned?"

Therefore, in developing appropriate questions, our first area of consideration is, "What kinds of questions should I formulate?" The answer is content, thought, and application questions.

To Whom Is the Question Directed?

A question can be directed in five different ways.*

a) The rhetorical question. For example, you might say, "You know what I mean, don't you?" or, "I'm sure you all agree, don't you?" Avoid rhetorical questions. They usually kill the discussion very quickly.

b) To one member of the group—the direct question. . . . Ask a specific individual to respond. "Joe, what did you learn from this chapter?" Direct questions are excellent when you want to draw out a quiet individual.

c) To the one who asked the previous question—the reverse question. . . . A member . . . might ask you as the leader, "Are you sure that is what that verse means?" . . . Don't answer, but rather reverse the question to the one who asked it by saying, "What do you think?" This type of question forces the questioner to think and express his own thoughts.

d) To the group, other than the previous questioner—the relay question. You are asked a question, and instead of answer-

*From "A Guide for Leadership Training and Bible Discussion Groups." © 1968 Billy Graham Evangelistic Association. Used by permission.

ing it you relay it back to the group as a whole. . . . Someone asks . . . "Can you explain what that verse means? I'm not sure I understand." You turn to the group by saying, "What do the rest of you think about that?" or, "Can anyone help him in understanding that verse?"

e) To the group as a whole—the general question. Instead of asking a direct question to one individual in the group, you are asking the question to anyone who wants to answer.

GUIDED DISCUSSION EXAMPLES

Whenever I have taught this material in conferences and seminars, I've included the following examples of how *not* to lead a guided discussion and how to lead a discussion. We tend to be impacted with the right way of doing things when we see it contrasted with the wrong way. Before you read the two scenarios, keep in mind the following pointers on "how to guarantee a *lousy* discussion":

1. Prepare inadequately.
2. Fail to create an atmosphere of freedom and ease.
3. Allow the discussion to wander aimlessly.
4. Dominate the discussion yourself.
5. Ask "yes" and "no" questions.
6. End the discussion without adequate application.
7. Become resentful and angry when people disagree with you.

With these seven points in mind along with the section "To whom is the question directed?" read the first example of how *not* to lead a guided discussion. In the margin, you may want to write the number of the principle that was violated.

HOW NOT TO LEAD A GUIDED DISCUSSION

Leader: I hope you've all read the first chapter of *Let's Live.** If it's anything like last week when just one of you completed the reading assignment, I'll really be dis-

---

*Curtis Mitchell, *Let's Live* (Old Tappan, N.J.: Revell, 1975). Used as illustration by author's permission.

appointed. I'm not going to ask you *now* whether you've read it; it will only frustrate me when I find out. So at the very end of our discussion, I want you to put on a piece of paper whether you've read the chapter or not, and if you *haven't* read it, I want you to put down two good reasons. And Dave, don't give me those same two reasons you gave me last week. But don't tell me now if you haven't read it. I'll only get mad. Just try to wing it through this discussion. It shouldn't take long anyway. It was kind of a boring chapter.

Now, first of all, isn't it true that Mitchell states that to most people Christianity is a very negative philosophy?

Tom: Yes.
Frank: Yes.
Dave: Yes.
Leader: And isn't it true that he meant by that that people tend to see the Christian in light of what he can't do or what shouldn't be done?
Tom: Yes.
Frank: Yes.
Dave: Yes.
Leader: Now I know that each of you has examples from your own life. Tom, you used to think that if a person doesn't smoke he must be a Christian. Right?
Tom: Yes.
Leader: And Frank, you used to think that if a person doesn't drink, he must be a Christian. Right?
Frank: Yes.
Dave: That reminds me of a guy I used to know. Boy, did he ever drink. He was always loaded.
Frank: Alcoholism is a real problem. There has to be answers to it. It ruins the individual who is drinking. It ruins the family unit. Just the other day I was reading in the paper about all the problems related to alcoholism.
Tom: That reminds me. I've always wanted to get the *Journal*. How much is it a month now?

Frank:	I can't remember, but it's worth it. I especially like the sports section.
Leader:	I think its time to get back to the issue at hand. I think our newspaper is great, but it has nothing to do with the point of this chapter. So let's zero in on the issue at hand.
	Maybe we could take this time to share the names of people we know who are struggling with a drinking problem.
Tom:	I'd like prayer for an individual by the name of Hank.
Frank:	My next-door neighbor, Bertha, needs prayer.
Dave:	Also Mike. He's a good friend of mine.
Leader:	Let's include Joe also.
	Anyway, Mitchell says Christianity is essentially positive. What does he mean by that?
Frank:	That we should always smile.
Leader:	Well, Frank, your ignorance has been revealed. It's obvious he's winging it. Anyone else have the *right* answer?
Tom:	In John 10:27-28, it says that Jesus *gives* us eternal life. A person who is a Christian is a person who has been *given* something by God. So it's positive.
Dave:	I didn't exactly understand his discusson on the meaning of eternal life. What exactly is it?
Leader:	I'll answer that one. Eternal life isn't simply existing forever. In John 17:3, Christ says, "And this is life eternal, that they might know thee the only true God, and Jesus Christ, whom thou hast sent." So eternal life is knowing God, knowing Jesus Christ.
Tom:	I'm not so sure that's the only thing involved.
Leader:	You know, Tom, you disagreed with me last week, and it took me three days to get over that. Now let me say it again—eternal life is knowing God.
	Now Mitchell states that the Bible pictures Christian living under several figures of speech or analogies. What are they? And I'm thinking of two in particular.
Frank:	Running the race.
Leader:	He mentioned that, Frank, but that's not one of the two I'm thinking of. Now, really think.

Dave:	Erecting a building.
Leader:	That's one.
Tom:	A little baby growing up.
Leader:	That's the other. All right! What was Mitchell's point in all this? [Pause] I forgot it too. That's OK; let's move on. Somewhere in his discussion, Mitchell talked about legalism.
Tom:	Oh, yeah, I remember.
Leader:	Did I ask for any comments? Now, somewhere he talked about legalism. Anyone remember the exact page number?
Frank:	Page seventeen?
Leader:	What do the rest of you think?
Tom:	Twenty-eight?
Leader:	Tom, have you been reading ahead? That's next week's chapter. What about you, Dave?
Dave:	I just can't remember.
Leader:	On page eighteen he talks about legalism.

You may be thinking that you have good Bible teaching along this line, and you may say you are no longer under law but under grace. Yet, I find that an awful lot of people who say that with their mouths are, in practice, living by law. They have fallen from grace. They really don't understanad what grace is all about.

Isn't this really the same philosophy that the Pharisees were following? They had reduced their religious experience to a little system of external dos and don'ts that they rigidly tried to follow. They would go to the synagogue at certain times, they would abstain from some kinds of meats, they would wash their hands a certain way, they would avoid some people, and their idea was to become ever more proficient at their little routine of dos and don'ts.

Now, the only difference between the Pharisees and many Christians today is that our dos and don'ts are different. The same basic philosophy is there. To become ever more proficient at your dos and don'ts, and become like a trained seal going through your little routine each week, is not authentic New Testament Christianity, but legalism. If there is anything that the Bible is against, it's legalism.

In fact, the book of Galatians points this out. Before we continue, I'd like to read to you the entire book of Galatians.

Tom: Do you have to? Last week you read us Leviticus.

Leader: Maybe you're right. Well, anyway, the last few pages of Mitchell's chapter, I'm sure, were significant. I ran out of time, so, I couldn't prepare. Dave, how about you taking over? I'll tell you what, let's just do our best to apply these truths.

It is hoped that the violations were obvious to you. Now read the following example for an idea of how a discussion should be led.

HOW TO LEAD A GUIDED DISCUSSION

Leader: You all read the first chapter of *Let's Live*, and I'm sure you noted that it's a very important chapter to understand regarding our walk with Christ. It basically emphasized the type of relationship we are to have with Christ and how we can build such a relationship.

First of all, Mitchell states that, to most people, Christianity is a very negative philosophy. What does he mean by that?

Tom: He means that people see the Christian life in light of what they can't do or what shouldn't be done.

Leader: Anyone have any examples—maybe from your own life or people you know?

Frank: One friend of mine says that if you don't smoke and if you don't drink, you're a Christian.

Dave: Yeah! One of my non-Christian friends says that he doesn't want to become a Christian because all he heard when he was a child was that he couldn't go to movies. Everything seemed to center on what he couldn't do. And he was told that a Christian wouldn't dare do those things. So he's had it with Christianity.

Leader: If that isn't the perspective we should have on the Christian life, why not?

Frank: Mitchell says that Christianity is a positive faith.

Leader: What does he mean by that—that Christian living is essentially positive?

Tom: In John 10:27-28, it says that Jesus *gives* us eternal life. A person who is a Christian is a person who has been *given* something by God. So it's positive.

Dave: I didn't exactly understand his discussion on the meaning of eternal life. What exactly is it?

Leader: What do the rest of you think?

Frank: Eternal life isn't simply existing forever. In John 17:3, Christ says, "And this is life eternal, that they might know thee the only true God, and Jesus Christ, whom thou has sent." So eternal life is knowing God, knowing Jesus Christ.

Tom: But there's also a difference between knowing about Jesus Christ and knowing Him. We can know facts about the life of Jesus Christ, but He wants us to know Him personally.

Leader: Exactly! And that's what Christianity is all about— it's a positive relationship—knowing Jesus Christ and getting to know Him better and better.

Mitchell states that the Bible pictures Christian living under several figures of speech or analogies. Anyone remember what they are?

Tom: In First Corinthians 3, Christian living is spoken of as a building program. When you receive Jesus Christ as Savior, it's like having the foundation of a building laid in place in your life, and Christian living is building a superstructure on top of that foundation.

Frank: He also said that Christian living is pictured as a growing process. You start out as a little baby, and you grow up.

Leader: What was Mitchell's point in all this?

Dave: If a man is going to erect a building, a contractor doesn't give his men a list of twelve things he doesn't want them to do. If they faithfully observed all of the don'ts, the building wouldn't go up.

Leader: And, Frank, what about the baby analogy?

Frank: If the mother wants her baby to grow healthy and strong, she doesn't list twelve things she isn't going to let her child experience. If that's all she did, the child would shrivel and die.

Leader: So what's the principle?

Tom: In the Christian life, ten thousand don'ts will never make us one bit more like Jesus Christ. We can't build positive Christlike character by don'ts.

Dave: Does that mean that we all have to get busy and do lot of positive things?

Leader: What do you think, Dave?

Dave: I don't think so. In fact, I remember that Mitchell used the illustration of Martha who was busy serving Christ, but she became harsh and bitter. Certainly in her case doing things for Christ didn't make her develop Christian character.

Frank: I can verify that. There are times when I've done a lot of religious activity but ended up only frustrated.

Leader: Then let me ask you this, Does it mean that we are to live our Christian lives by a *combination* of dos and don'ts?

Tom: Do you mean by that that we rigidly follow a routine of dos and don'ts?

Leader: Yes. Is that what we're to do? Is that what makes a successful Christian life? Observing all of our dos and abstaining from all our don'ts?

Dave: That's legalism.

Leader: What's wrong with that, Dave?

Dave: The Christian life is not a legal relationship but a love relationship.

Leader: What is the difference between a legal relationship and a love relationship?

Frank: Is that the same thing as living under law and living under grace?

Leader: What do the rest of you think?

Tom: Yes, it is, and the difference is not what you do or don't do, but the motivation—why you do what you do. A legal relationship is motivated by fear and reward.

Leader: What would be an example of that from your own lives?

Tom: At my job, I do what I do because I'm afraid I'll get fired.

Leader: And what about grace?

Frank: Grace is motivated by love. Mitchell used the illustration of a housemaid and a housewife. Both the housemaid and housewife make the beds, do the dishes, and mop the floors. They do the same tasks, but the difference is the motivation. The housemaid is operating under legal contract. If she doesn't do her job well, she'll get fired. But the housewife does these things because she loves her husband and family.

Leader: How does that apply to us?

Tom: If I read my Bible today because I thought, *That's what a good Christian does* or because I was afraid of what God would do to me if I didn't, then it would be a legal relationship, not a love relationship.

Dave: It's so easy to do things in the Christian life motivated out of fear.

Leader: Is that what the Lord would want?

Dave: Not at all.

Leader: What is our basic task in Christian life?

Frank: Our basic task is to maintain a high level love relationship between ourselves and the Lord Jesus.

Leader: And what is the key or secret of maintaining a love relationship?

Tom: Communication. You have to communicate with a person to stay in love with that person.

Dave: And that means that the issue isn't, Am I reading my Bible everyday? but rather, Am I communicating by this process?

Leader: How should a Christian view such disciplines as prayer, Bible study, and public worship?

Tom: They should be viewed as a means to an end—means by which we communicate.

Leader: Mitchell suggests four keys to communication. What are these, and why is each important?

Frank: One is desire. For two people to stay in love with each other, they must want to. In our Christian life we must want to know Christ more and more. Paul

	said that he had a desire to press on toward the mark.
Dave:	Another is confidence. If two people are going to communicate with each other, they have to have confidence in each other. And with Christ, we need to have faith in Him. Galatians two twenty says, "I have been crucified with Christ; and it is no long I who live, but Christ lives in me; and the life which I now live in the flesh I live by faith in the Son of God, who loved me, and delivered Himself up for me."
Leader:	Tom, what is another key to communication?
Tom:	Commitment. For two people to remain in love, they need to be dedicated to each other. Romans twelve one says, "I beseech you therefore brethren, by the mercies of God, that you present your bodies a living sacrifice, holy, acceptable unto God, which is your reasonable service."
Leader:	And the last?
Frank:	Honesty. Dishonesty destroys a love relationship. With the Lord, we need to confess our sins.
Leader:	Now let's each answer a question, and as we do let's write down each person's response so we can close in prayer for that person. The question is this: Of these four keys to communication, the one that is weakest in my life is _____. And after we share our own answer, let's share one thing we can do this week to help strengthen that area.

EPILOGUE

What am I doing that can ultimately have an impact on this world? What am I doing that will have eternal consequences? In the first chapter I stated that I had asked myself those questions when evaluating my life and goals. The answer drove me to a discipling ministry. I had to become involved in that which counted. My life had to be given to that which is significant. I wanted to have an impact, not only on my own generation, but also on generations to come. For that to occur, I needed to make a commitment to people.

A friend of mine named Mike made such a commitment. As a university student he had a fruitful ministry, leading a dormitory Bible study. He taught and counseled and began discipling men. While Mike was attending seminary, doctors discovered that he was suffering from a terminal illness. Did Mike make an impact? Ask Steve, who is now pastoring a church in Los Angeles. Ask Ralph, who, involved in a sports ministry, is sharing his faith and living his life to God's glory. Ask John, who is now involved in a reproduction ministry. These men would emphatically say, "Yes!" They are products of Mike's ministry. They are continuing the task entrusted to them by Mike, discipling others whom God leads in their direction. They are trophies of Mike's life and labor. That is fulfillment! Mike's was a life given to that which is eternal.

What about you? Is what *you* are doing likely to have lasting impact on this world? What are *you* doing that will have eternal consequences? Can you say that *your* life is counting now? Are *you* investing your life in the lives of people? To what are you giving yourself? I trust that your answers will drive you, as mine drove me, to the ministry of discipling others.